The Tribulations of a Sahelian Traveler

Published by Michel Tinguiri

Published in the USA by Michel Tinguiri

First edition

ISBN-13: 978-0615981697
ISBN-10: 0615981690

DEDICATION

To Assetou Barry, Binta Tinguiri and Mariam Tinguiri

Table of Contents

Foreword by Professor Christopher Wise

I first met Michel Tinguiri nearly twenty years ago, while he was still a student at the Université de Ouagadougou in Burkina Faso in 1996. At that time, Michel assisted me in research projects on various Sahelian writers, including the Malian novelist Yambo Ouologuem and the Peulh sage Al Hajj Sekou Tall. It was a turbulent year in Ouagadougou with university students on strike and a growing disenchantment with the culture of impunity and governmental corruption prevailing in the nation's capital. Among other topics, the famed journalist Norbert Zongo wrote about the student strike in his journal L'Indépendant -- he had not yet been assassinated by three members of the Presidential Guard -- and many Burkinabe still grieved for Capitain Thomas Sankara, who'd been slain in a coup d'état a few years earlier. Michel was enormously helpful to me at this time; and, knowing his gifts as a scholar and translator, I strongly encouraged him to pursue graduate studies in the United States. Michel and his lovely wife Assetou eventually relocated to the U.S., where in time he earned his Ph.D. in Cultural Anthropology at the American University in Washington, D.C. Meanwhile, Michel and I continued to collaborate on various projects, including our joint translation of Ouologuem's satiric work, A Black Ghostwriter's Letter to France.

It has been an honor and pleasure to work with Michel over the years and to witness his courage and perseverance in overcoming many obstacles in reaching his goals, both personal and professional. Though Michel studied for several years in Ouagadougou, he was born in a small village in northern Burkina Faso where he experienced many of the hardships described in The Tribulations of a Sahelian Traveler. For those who have never visited the Sahel, it may be difficult to imagine day-to-day life in such a harsh and unforgiving environment, a desert landscape that the Burkinabe poet Titinga Frédérick Pacéré once called "homicidal."

Having grown up in a humble village on the edge of the Sahara, Michel knows from personal experience the great urgency of the problems that his people confront.

Readers in the West who are accustomed to novels featuring individual heroes, the intrepid adventurer who faces the world on his own, may feel somewhat disoriented by the collective life described in The Tribulations of a Sahelian Traveler. In the Sahel, no one can possibly survive on his or her own. No matter how resolute the man, no isolated individual can pull himself up by his own bootstraps. Instead, human survival depends upon collective existence, upon the necessity of honoring one's vows and responsibilities to others. As the griot of Lafidougou proclaims in Michel's novel, "we need others to survive the bitter and unpredictable contours of life and existence... A person is not a person without others." Though Michel's novel is about a single Sahelian traveler, the hero N'Djilékou is not a solitary man but an important member of his community, a village facing challenges that are unimaginable for readers in the developed world. The wisdom articulated in Michel's novel is the wisdom of an ancient civilization and collective society.

With the publication of this novel, Michel takes his place among important Burkinabe writers like Patrice Ilboudo, Norbert Zongo, Titinga Pacéré, Joseph Ki-Zerbo, Al Hajj Sekou Tall, and many others. There is, however, something that distinguishes him from this illustrious group: Michel has written his novel in English, not French. This makes him Burkina Faso's first English language novelist. I look forward to seeing what else he'll write in the years to come.

The Chiefs' Whims: Cotton, the Road and the Dam

Aunt Pèlo was sitting under a baobab tree in front of her old mud-built house. She was staring at her cotton spindle. The bead was made up of black and white color lines. Next to her, there was some cotton piled in a huge basket.

Aunt Pèlo's face showed joy and satisfaction as she spun her cotton and sang in a low key voice. From time to time, she dipped her thumb and forefinger into some ashes in a ceramic plate, and then again grabbed the upper terminal of the spindle with agility and in slow motion, she spun the spindle clockwise. You could see the cotton thread being gently created and taking shape, rolling around at the base above the ceramic bead.

Aunt Pèlo could spend hours sitting under the baobab, just spinning her cotton. She loved it and made all her family clothes herself. Cotton and cotton spinning had become part of her life. Sometimes, other elders joined her, and together, they spent their time talking or sometimes singing while spinning.

In the village, as women grew older, they took care of their grandchildren, tended a small peanut garden, or spent their time spinning cotton. They believed that spinning cotton enabled them to spend their lives in a meaningful manner. That was one of the ways for them to help their families. Since the introduction of cotton cultivation, women had begun to have their small gardens. They combined cotton crops with peanut, peas, beans and corn. Such variation allowed them to earn some money for their basic household needs. Aunt Pèlo was proud of spinning cotton as it allowed her to spend quality time with her friends and also to meet her children's basic needs.

As Aunt Pèlo was busy spinning her cotton, her grandson Kô stepped out of the compound and went to greet her. After talk of the weather, he sat on an old stool next to her. Kô was a funny and hardworking adolescent. He loved to tinker around. He was known as the most talented artist of his generation in the village. Kô hadn't completed primary school. He dropped out in the fifth grade and learned to be self-reliant at an early age. He loved drawing, making designs on chairs, on traditional pots and calabashes and reading comic books. He made several comic books by himself in notebooks, and sold them to primary school students. He spent his time making art objects, traditional musical instruments, and hoes that he sold at the local market for a couple of cowries. As Kô sat next to aunt Pèlo, her face lightened up even more, and then she asked him, "So, how is your day?"

"Ah, not so bad; it could be better." Kô replied.

"Stop playing with words with me. Tell me what's bothering you."

"Nothing," Kô deflected the question and said, "You really love spinning cotton. And you're also a great weaver. I don't know if I can spin cotton like you, but I'd really love to become a weaver; I mean a great weaver just like you."

"A weaver?" she asked in a tone of surprise.

"Yeah, a weaver," he replied with a grin at the corner of his mouth.

Aunt Pèlo just sighed as if she were trying to keep something to herself. And then she added, "I learned to weave from N'Djilékou, my cousin. He was a great weaver and great man too. His name reflected his character. Yes, N'Djilékou means Self-control. He was calm and poised, always."

"By the way, who was he?" Kô asked.

"You have always been so inquisitive. Since you want to hear more about his story, so let me tell you a little bit about him," Aunt Pèlo added.

"So, who was he exactly?" Kô asked.

After a pause, Aunt Pèlo continued, "as I told you a little while ago, N'Djilékou is my cousin. He was hardworking, a brave and respectful person. I was younger than him. He taught me many things, including weaving. He married Banko and they had three beautiful children: Banambonon, Gontan and Pèret. Life was getting tougher. Yes, the situation got worse. Many things led to this chaos. Cotton was one of the root causes of our problems.

"Really?" Kô asked.

"Yes," Aunt Pèlo replied. "Cotton brought us both good and bad things. N'Djilékou had become increasingly dissatisfied with how things were unfolding in the village. You know, in the past, we didn't grow cotton that much. Very few people cultivated cotton just to make some cloth to cover themselves or for specific needs such as burial cloth. They used to bring cloth from far away, from Bamanandougou. Then, the *lansara*, the white people, imposed cotton cultivation. At the beginning, people were eager because the village chief gathered all the elders and told them that by growing cotton, they would improve their livelihoods and have better crops. He said that cotton would bring us more money and goods from the land of the *lansara*. And the people applauded. And they believed him because he was the chief."

"What about N'Djilékou?" Kô asked.

"N'Djilékou was among the first people who decided to give it a try. The first year, he harvested a lot of cotton, and sold it, and earned a

15

lot of cowries with which he paid taxes, including those for his brothers and uncles. But things quickly turned sour when the *lansara* began to force people to go and farm on the chief's cotton fields. The second year, N'Djilékou's entire cotton income went into paying taxes. He didn't get anything. We didn't understand why our people should be forced to work for nothing.

Then, the chief said that the *lansara* people were fighting a big war in their land, and that we had to show our support by helping with cotton. But, we still didn't understand why we should be forced to grow cotton to fight a war so far away. How could you use cotton to fight? And we said that a true friend doesn't pick a fight and then force you to fight. We asked why our friends picked up a war they couldn't fight alone. Now they were asking us to join them in a fight that we didn't even start in the first place. It wasn't our fight. Anyway, people began to be frustrated when the chief started to take away their fertile lands to grow cotton. People were forced to give up their lands. They were also beaten by the guards and taken to jail. They had to spend at least one day of forced labor on the chief's cotton farm.

To make things worse, there was Sègué, a local guard, so wicked and mean! He would tie people's feet and then drag them in the streets just to shame them. He would shave their head and make them crawl into the mud in front of their wives and children any time that they failed to go to work on the chief's farm.

People suffered the same fate when they couldn't afford to pay their taxes. Life just became more and more bitter. People sometimes were arbitrarily arrested for three to five weeks, sometimes during the rainy season. On their farms, the grasses grew higher and higher and even destroyed some of their crops. When they finally came out of jail, they had to struggle to cultivate their own farms. All this happened for ten solid years, and during those years, the world became unbearable for all of us. Our lands became poorer and they couldn't even produce peanuts anymore. As a result, harvests were meager. Some people believed all this was due to the curse of cotton.

Others said it was the greed of the authorities who started farming on the sacred lands.

Many people had to travel thirty kilometers away from the village to farm because the lands closer to the village became unproductive or they were taken by cotton. It was so exhausting to travel such a distance. In the end, some decided to live on their farms. They left the village. People left the village and went to Bamanandougou in the North, or down south towards the sea in Felikro and Sanandougou.

"What about N'Djilékou?" Kô asked.

Aunt Pèlo answered, "N'Djilékou used to own a farm in the wetland. It was the only thing that held him in the village. He continued to farm there. But then, one rainy season, his uncle Logo suddenly claimed that the land belonged to his great grandfather. He therefore wanted it back. It turned into a fight. N'Djilékou was a gentleman who never liked fighting. He didn't pick the fight. His uncle had picked the fight out of jealousy. He slapped N'Djilékou. And N'Djilékou slapped him back. Then, they took the matter to the chief's court. And the chief decided to keep the land for himself. He decided to farm cotton there. Not food, but cotton. It was the only fertile land left for N'Djilékou. He was very disappointed by the chief's decision. You see, many other things happened.

Then, as people started losing their lands, the district commander decided to build the road to the capital, Mogodougou. The road was another disaster for us. We didn't ask for it. Yet we were forced to work to build it. So, we didn't understand why we should build a road to the city when we didn't travel there. The road also made a lot of victims in our village and in the surrounding villages too. When someone was recruited by force to go work on the road, family members would cry as if the person were dead. And indeed, the road took many lives.

The guards would come and force people to go and dig the laterite quarry to build the earthen road to Mogodougou. That was very dreadful. The young people were forced to dig the laterite, sometimes under the scorching sun. Failing to do so resulted in humiliation and incarceration. Horrible things started to happen at the laterite quarry site. One day, the laterite quarry collapsed and about seven young people lost their lives. The wounded were screaming out of pain, dreadful pain. It was a real tragedy. People said the gods of the sacred land were taking revenge against the violation of their territory, and the killing and maiming of their family members. According to local diviners, the laterite diggers had killed a baby spirit. So, its mother and father were so angry that they decided to take revenge by pushing down the laterite walls on the quarry workers. That revenge was the straw that broke the camel's back.

N'Djilékou had a narrow escape. When the quarry collapsed, he was resting under a tree. It was his turn to rest. He was woken from his sleep by the loud grumbling sound and screams all over the place. He woke up shaking. Then, they had to do something to rescue the victims. It was a terrible scene. They tried to retrieve the survivors, maimed bodies, and those who couldn't make it out of the rubble. The tragedy really affected N'Djilékou.

As if that were not enough, the governor decided to build a dam to connect Ganda-Gulo to Bamanandougou. He said the supreme leader of his mother country in the White man's land, wanted to develop cotton farm on the Joliba River. And we said, "To build a dam in Markadougou and to challenge the spirits of Joliba! The Great Joliba River! That was really too much." However, our people couldn't stop the supreme leader of the *lansara* people from doing what he wanted to do. He said he was going to build a dam and he was going to do it no matter what! Rain or shine.

So, on one sunny day, the commander sent a messenger to the chief to inform him about his decision to build the dam. Then, he sent out *djeliba*, the griot, to announce the news in the main market place, then in every major gathering site in the village. I still remember that day as if it were just yesterday."

"You always amazed me with your great memory!" Kô said while smiling.

"Well, memory is what makes us you know. We can't forget things and people that shaped our lives. But, we tend to forget things these days." Aunt Pèlo replied.

Kô admitted, "Yes, I agree memory makes us. I agree."

Aunt Pèlo then went on with her narrative. "So, as I was saying, when we got the news, we were all saddened because we knew that was a terrible message. It was just getting too much for us. First, it was about cultivating cotton, and then we lost our lands, and our young people. Then, the road came, and again, we lost our lands and our young people. Then the dam; another thing forced upon us. We didn't ask for it. The building of Markadougou's dam took away our lands, some of our young people too; and even worse, seven villages were wiped out by the waters of Joliba.

The commander recruited by force young people. They spent months working there, and when they were lucky, they returned home, severely affected and completely transformed. N'Djilékou spent six months in Markadougou. Our ancestors and the gods protected him. Before his departure, he consulted the oracle, who told him that would return home safe and sound. And he returned home safe and sound. However, not everybody was as lucky as N'Djilékou."

The saddest news was when parents received "a basket containing their son's clothes."

That was the symbol and a message that their son hadn't survived the dam. Some fell into the waters of the Great Joliba River and they never reappeared. It was their end. The river "ate them," people said. When Markadougou's dam was finished, the waters inundated farms and neighboring villages. Hundreds of families were swept away by the raging waters of the Great Joliba River.

People lost their lands, and their cemeteries and sacred mangroves were all taken away by the dam. People said that the god of the river was mad because Markadougou's dam was built on his palace. He couldn't take that humiliation. Every now and then, he would push the waters to flood all the lands and neighboring villages. The big flood was followed by cholera that killed children and adults. It was horrific. Every now and then, he would spit fire rising from the waters and burning the green trees and grasses around.

A year after the construction of the dam, Gonku, the great diviner announced the coming of two major droughts and the drying up of the Joliba River. He said that the Great Snake of the Joliba

River wanted to take revenge against the violation and humiliation of his people. The Great Snake promised to fill up the Joliba River with sand and to bring wars among the people. The Great Snake promised to turn brothers and sisters against each other for generations to come. He promised to bring warriors from the North, warriors from the South, and warriors from the East and West to fight to free his land.

When N'Djilékou returned, he couldn't stop talking about the waters flowing and grumbling like thunders. People said that it was the big river snake preparing his weapon to wage a war against the workers. He kept talking about the Joliba's waters becoming red like blood, and many people who caught foot-diseases due to unknown germs from the mud left behind after floods. After torrential rains, the waters would flood nearby villages and farms.

A year later, N'Djilékou decided that it was time for him to leave the village in search of peace. Yes, N'Djilékou left and relocated to Lafidougou to find better opportunities for his family. Now, I spin my cotton and weave when I can.

As, I told you, I learned to weave from N'Djilékou. I learned to get the most out of what I learned from him."

Memories: Fragmentation and Tribulations

N'Djilékou still remembered the death of Tobri and the subsequent events that affected the whole life of the extended family, and that of the entire neighborhood. He also remembered the scars left by cotton, the road and the dam. Gonku's prophecy about the major droughts came true. N'Djilékou witnessed and saw it all.

Ever since the passing of Tobri, life had become dull for the Yiri family. Tobri was one of the survivors of the quarry collapse. He also had a fall during the building of Markadougou's dam. Ever since that fall, he had suffered from backache and respiratory issues. While his death was perceived as a tragedy because he was the unifying figure of the extended family, it didn't come as a big surprise. Everybody knew that his fall and the dust he had inhaled at the construction site had severely affected him.

Since his death, the compounds were shrouded by an awful silence. He was the symbol of power, unification and hope. The extended family members began to wonder whether there would be someone of his stature that would unite the people and the family. He was the source of energy that allowed them to fight defeatism, and to imagine other possibilities.

Brothers were at each other's throats. Reciprocity became a vain word. The law of the jungle prevailed. No peace, no generosity, in short, no brotherhood.

Evil was destroying the heart of the community, and even the great diviners could not stop its expansion. The whole community lost it; no guide! Society was sad. Life was moody. Everybody was apathetic; everybody became a cold observer of the community falling apart. Fragmentation!

N'Djilékou recalled all the tribulations that his village and his people had gone through: cotton, the road and the dam. He also still recalled that, seven years ago, the entire region had been affected by a severe drought and a terrible famine. People from neighboring villages ran away in search of food, water and shelter. Animals and humans dropped like flies. Even clean drinking water was very scarce.

Those running from the starvation were especially coming from the north, and they were migrating to the south where rains were abundant and where people had enough to eat so that they even fed their horses and donkeys with sorghum and corn. After that famine was over, people were no longer themselves after having eaten leaves and grasses and anything edible, just like animals, to survive.

Shortly before the independence of Ganda-Gulo, the region was also affected by a severe drought and a subsequent famine, but it was very quickly controlled because free foodstuffs and drinking water were distributed to villagers, and health care was provided for free.

Then, the great famine struck. The local authorities did not care at all about the people.

They even tried to hide the famine from the outside world. They said they had everything under control while people and their pets were dying by the hundreds. Those who had enough strength and energy to run away, did so, whether on horseback, camel or even donkey backs, or on foot. They took with them what they could take. Vultures followed them, flying above them, expecting them to fall somewhere along their trip. Indeed, some fell by the roadside and did not rise again. They were buried helter-skelter and the rest of the group continued their way to the south. The picture was appalling and heartbreaking. Some of them were so drained by hunger after several days of forced fasting to the point that when they were given food and drink, they could barely eat. They threw up and became weaker. They often fainted for lack of food and drinking water.

Help was not coming because there was no real help available. Victims had no means of communication to call for rescue. Worse, the local authorities sometimes refused to see and to hear some of the desperate calls for assistance. Instead, they scrambled to hide the truth and the misery of their people to avoid criticism from the international community.

Reportedly, the village prefect, including his henchmen embezzled foodstuffs and drugs originally meant for Tiala and its neighboring villages. They lined their own pockets and accumulated more wealth and power at the expense of the people. The village prefect became richer and even built villas in his native village, Wara. He built up his fortune on the misery and desolation of the people. At the height of the crisis, he travelled regularly to Mogodougou – the capital city of Ganda-Gulo – to seek for assistance. But when humanitarian organizations provided a little help, he kept it for himself. He did not really care about the fate of the community.

So the plague revealed the evil side of those who said they were fighting for the development of their people and the region, those who claimed to be fighting for the welfare of the community. That bitter pill was too bitter to swallow, and the memories were so bitter to be soon forgotten. That was why there was no real trust between the people and the local authorities, and sometimes among the people themselves.

The late crisis was mismanaged both by the national and local authorities. No mechanism was set up to prevent the disaster. Some local Non-Governmental Organizations' representatives also seized the opportunity to amass fortune. While people were dying or running away for their lives, some NGO leaders were busy organizing extravagant parties with friends and buying new cars and scooters. It was a real insult to the people; a slap in the face. With such behavior, people stopped trusting their authorities and so-called development NGOs. It was more about accumulation.

N'Djilékou vividly recalled that the first great famine was even better managed and did not wreak such havoc and trauma. Together with foreign experts, the national government set up cereal banks' management systems. The cereal banks were used for emergency assistance.

Before the big famine, so-called "development agents" roamed villages to sensitize farmers on new farming techniques for the improvement of agricultural productivity. However, the villagers did not understand much about the message they were trying to convey because they were talking to them in a language that they did not understand. Jargons, jargons, nothing but jargons! Worse, when some of the agents used local translators, the message was convoluted and the interactions with the villagers ended up in laughter, laughter expressing despair. As a result, the villagers never took them seriously and kept farming as their grandfathers used to do. There was no real change in farming techniques. No change at all.

However, when the second great famine hit, people expected the government to use existing cereal banks to rescue them while waiting for external assistance. It never happened. Instead, when the crisis broke out, which was no surprise; local and national authorities rather plundered local cereal banks and sold them in other parts of the country. They brought vans at night to empty the cereal banks. They took all the cereals to unknown destination.

Yet, there were early warning signs of the famine. When the young plants started dying for lack of rain, followed by the invasion of crickets, everybody knew that the harvests would be a total disaster. Everybody anticipated that disaster.

However, despite all this natural warning system, both the national and local authorities took no further steps to mitigate the effects of the drought and to cope with the cricket infestation. The villagers knew that life was going to be harsher for them, but they thought that with the cereal banks in place, they would be able to fill up the gap while waiting for the next rainy season to come. That was a mere illusion. And they learned it the hard way.

At the very beginning of the crisis, the local authorities showed some positive signs of concern by distributing fifty kilograms of red sorghum to each household. But that was it! They abandoned the people to their own fate.

That severe drought and its subsequent famine created a real trauma among the people. Solidarity and trust became empty words. Evil grew in strength and attacked everything. Families were broken, they fell apart. Each member left like a dry leaf and was dragged away by the wind, gone and gone away. They forgot that unity makes force and that life is to be built on solidarity, generosity and cordiality. They lost the essence of life, the substance that makes life: solidarity, care and love. Selfishness and blind egotism took over. So, they lost everything.

In Mogodougou, the capital city, life was even worse. Nobody really wanted to go to Mogodougou, because rumors had it that life there, was even worse than in the village. People had to sleep on the streets plagued with violence and all sorts of diseases. The new comers to the city often became beggars, and they had to scavenge the rubbish piles to get their daily bread.

That was why Yiri N'Djilékou decided to go to Lafidougou instead. He decided to go away to explore other opportunities. That was why he had to go. That was why he had decided to go. N'Djilékou strongly believed that sometimes, one must listen to one's inner voice. And the voice told him in his dream that he should go.

The Voice

You saw the seeds of cotton that brought you short-lived joy, chimera, and false hopes. You heard and experienced Gonku's prophecy about the two major droughts. You saw the road that came to you and took your lands, tore the heart of your lands and inflicted pain that ran deep in your spine, and ate your soul slowly. And you saw the dam that uprooted you and your people, the dam that tore apart the palace of the Great Snake of the Joliba River, the dam that took your lands and showed the seeds of chaos. You saw the waters of the Joliba River become red like blood and the waters that steamed and flooded your lands and villages. You saw injustice disguised like the law of the land. And you experienced the brutality of the law that turned against you and your people. You saw the rogue leaders using the law to destroy you and your people. You saw the rogue leaders using the law to muzzle the people. And when you asked them "what kinds of law destroys and oppresses people?" You were constantly told, "It is the law. We cannot challenge the law. We are sorry. We understand your pain and your trauma. But it is the law. We cannot discuss the brutality of the law. We just have to follow the law. And you shouldn't even seek to understand it because the law says that we cannot talk about it. We must continue to apply the law. We know it hurts you, but we have to hurt you for the common good and for the law." You saw it all. Didn't I, the Great Guardian of your land, tell you all that in your dreams? I am the echo, the voice of silence, the mother of all rivers whose waters flow endlessly. Dams cannot stop the flow of my waters. Only silence can hear my voice and my words.

In every human life, there are times to make crucial decisions: to choose or not to choose, to take charge of one's destiny or to leave it in the hands of others, to live, to grow, to become, or of course to die.

Ideas kept on boggling N'Djilékou's mind these days. He had to make a decision. But he was confused because he knew that migrating could both have positive and negative impacts on his life and that of his entire family. However, he had to make the decision to go. Going elsewhere, exploring the unknown, learning to grow had always been crucial for N'Djilékou. But he had to fight against the hindering forces around him and beyond.

N'Djilékou was silent. A strange, yet familiar voice said, "Never sit down and fold up your arms, curl up and die like an animal. You should always take your own initiatives. You should grow beyond yourself and know your limits and capabilities. You should know when and how to throw in the towel or when to move on. Learn to fight and learn to win. That's why you must choose, because if you do not choose, others will do it for you at your own risks and perils. So you have to choose to be or not to be, to become what you have always wished from the bottom of your heart or give up and fade away.

Do not always expect people to make the right choice for you. You know, look at Nature. Do you know how to read the language of Mother Nature? Look at ants! They are always energetic and busy. Very busy indeed! Despite their size, despite being tiny, they are fighting. Look at migratory birds, they know when to migrate and they know where they are going. Look around you and closely observe Nature. Everything is dynamic. Everything is recreation, invention and reinvention. That's why you should understand; you should understand and accept what you hear now.

Do not resist for the sake of resistance, because this will be a fruitless effort that will take you nowhere. Everything is dynamic in this universe. And you should move positively towards the fulfillment of your being. Nobody else will save you if you sit down doing nothing. That's why you should understand this world and know when and how to move accordingly. Humans are what they are and they will always be unpredictable; complex beings. But make no mistake, though humans are complex, they still shift sides, they become, they change colors, they invent and reinvent themselves.

They reveal themselves, and they also hide themselves. So, move on with your life. Be yourself! Get rid of the slave mentality.

Be creative and self-reliant. You should stand up and fight for your life, your dignity and your rights. Never let anybody trample underfoot your dignity in the name of the law."

Departing: Exploring New Possibilities

That evening, the weather was beautiful and sunny. You could hear a needle drop. You could even hear a fly buzzing around. There were still some clouds on the horizon. Birds were resting in the trees and some poor insects were bumping into the wall of the central house. N'Djilékou came out of his house smiling and sat on a stool under the common shed of the compound.

A cool wind was blowing and everybody was enjoying the fresh air. Nobody was speaking. This silence was the expression of the general tense atmosphere that affected the life of the whole compound. Then, N'Djilékou cleared his throat to inform his extended family and the elders about his decision to leave. Suddenly, Pengo, his cousin, got up and angrily howled, "I was born here, I grew up here and I will live my last days here. Go wherever you want. Going away will not make you better than us! Am I clear enough?"

N'Djilékou replied, "Of course, you ARE! I understand where you are coming from and what you are saying. Don't worry about that. God will protect me, and I will live in peace. Remember that we're all travelers in this world. Our ancestors came from somewhere to settle in this village to achieve their goals. I am going because I need to find better opportunities for myself and for my family. I feel stifled. Remember, cursing is not the solution. If you can't care or don't care, do not curse. Don't you know that the world is based on Love? Let me tell you then! I will go. Yes, I will go to learn to live in peace. Life is empty here. Don't worry about my going away."

Then, the patriarch, Zèrè, an old man with a curved back, gray hair and calloused feet took the floor and said, "Yes, to retreat on the battlefield has never kept the courageous warrior from winning the battle. This is rather a sign of wisdom. You should run away from evil when necessary and get ready to better face it. Such is life. But, when you run away from evil, you should remember it because it may follow you, as your shadow does. Yes! My son, go in peace. May God bless you, may our ancestors protect you in all your actions.

Nonetheless, you should know that the world is complex and that it changes like a chameleon. Everywhere, there is evil. Humans have a lot in common wherever they are. You can only know them partially. In every human, you can find the devil. In every human, you can find good and bad. Don't try by all means to do what you cannot do, don't impose your will when there's no need to do so. I cannot leave the village. I have experienced better days, great times in my life. I can hear my ancestors' call. When I was about your age, I never thought of leaving the village. Our time was better, but today, things have changed. The world has turned upside down. That's why you should go away while you can still do so. N'Djilékou, do not listen to what does not feed your soul and your mind. People always look for ways and means to hinder the development of their kind. You should be able to see the difference between what is wrong and what is right. Lies are foggy and nauseous. But truth is plain like daylight, and every truth comes straight. Remember that my son. Remember that."

"Thank you Papa Zèrè," N'Djilékou added. "We have already packed all our stuffs. Tomorrow, my family and I will be heading to Lafidougou."

N'Djilékou was a smart and courageous gentleman who had been raised by a family that believed in truth, dignity and self-respect and the respect of others. When he was about seven years old, he stood tall from his childhood playmates through his skills and smartness. Many admired him: men, women and children. Adults used to call him "my son." Yet, the crisis had fragmented all these things that used to hold them together. N'Djilékou wanted to leave to preserve what could be preserved, and to reinvent himself.

As the elders used to say, an honest man born in a family promotes the social status of that family. An honest and honorable child, a *den-horon* will always fight for justice and dignity. But an obnoxious and shameless man, totally devoid of dignity, brings sorrows and disgrace to the family.

Such children use the law to punish their parents and communities. Yet, a *den-horon* becomes everybody's child and promotes their parents' name in the community and beyond. N'Djilékou was a *den-horon*.

* * *
*

With the first songs of the roosters, N'Djilékou woke up. Darkness still shrouded the village. The angel of God had not yet removed its mysterious veil over the village. N'Djilékou recalled a story which held that everything spoke at night.

In fact, it was said that the night was full of mysteries; that sacred trees moved and went to chat with their friends. Spirits wandered and played during the night. Stones, insects, everything spoke. The elders used to say that the wind spoke, and that this world was full of sibylline messages that everybody may not understand. His ancestors used to say that when you violate Mother Nature's laws, the gods and spirits react in a harsh way. They say that you don't start planting without performing sacrifices to request the help and blessing of the gods, spirits and ancestors. You don't harvest without performing sacrifices. You don't hunt without asking the permission from the ancestors and the spirits of the bush. When asked why, the answer was always, "it's tradition, it's *n'yé-yiranè*," meaning that they "were born and found it." You don't challenge *n'yé-yiranè* without offending the gods, the spirits and the ancestors.

N'Djilékou mumbled something and slipped back under his blanket. A bit later, he opened his eyes and realized that the sky was getting lighter and lighter. He got up quickly and woke his wife, Banko. Together, they got ready for their trip. First, each took a bath, and then they ate millet porridge. Later, N'Djilékou went to inform his brothers and the compound's patriarch about their departure for Lafidougou. They wished him well. The patriarch said, "Wherever you go, you should know that you left your brothers and sisters behind. You should not forget us. You should not forget them. Do not forget your roots because without roots you are nothing. No breathing souls forget their roots. Don't forget your roots. May God bless you, may our ancestors protect you."

N'Djilékou thanked them and joined his spouse, Banko and their daughter Banambonon. Banambonon was eleven years old. She was shy, yet very active and creative. Weeks before the departure, her mother informed her that they were going to relocate to a great village where she would make new great friends. She asked her mother, whether she could invite her favorite friend Saa to join them. Her mother replied that Saa would be visiting them from time to time and that they would also do the same. Her mother reassured her and even promised that they would occasionally be returning to Tiala to see Banambonon's friends. Banambonon was sad and a bit anxious too. She loved playing with her friends and she didn't know whether her new friends would like her. On the eve of their departure, Banambonon helped her mother pack up. She insisted on taking her favorite she-goat Nana with her. Both parents quickly agreed. Their main concern was to make sure that Banambonon was not disturbed at all by their relocation to Lafidougou.

After the farewell, the family started the hard and long journey. They had two donkeys loaded with their luggage. Banambonon was on the back of the gentle female donkey. They left the main compound and headed southwest to Lafidougou.

The sun began to shine brightly. On the horizon, some clouds were moving slowly and accumulating, which foreshadowed rainfall. Farther away, birds were singing, jumping from branch to branch and from tree to tree. On their way, N'Djilékou told stories to while away the time. He listened to their melodious songs and interpreted them for his wife. But, she hardly answered him. So, he realized that resting was necessary for his wife to regain her strength for the remainder of the journey. They rested under the shade of a tree by the roadside.

As they were sitting, Banko took out a gourd and gulped down some fresh water. Then, she passed it around. Everybody drank to their fill. Banko sighed and started to scan the sky and suddenly, she hummed: "huum uhum!"

"What's the matter?" N'Djilékou asked.
Banko sighed and said, "Just remembrances that keep bothering me. Perhaps, you still remember. Once, our daughter Banambonon beat our neighbor's. Without even trying to understand the

reasons for their dispute, she verbally attacked us. She insulted my grandparents, my brothers and sisters, I mean, all the family. She was so spiteful like a wolf. She spoke very badly that day. She was fed by wickedness. Well, she did not spare anyone. She was simply terrible and terribly simple-minded. She was physically and morally ugly and would even win the ugliest prize. I'm sorry to speak about her that way, but that was what she was."

"I see," N'Djilékou replied.

Then Banko went on, "Her life became really miserable. She eventually became a beggar. And worse, everyone rejected her. Guess what though? She called me all the names. However, I would still welcome her in our home and I would give her food and drink. And she would go back home, apparently shameless. Ah! Life! 'Wonders will never end,' they say. To live better, to live peacefully and in harmony with others, it is vital to reduce, if not get rid of selfishness, pride and wickedness. Wickedness does not pay, or it pays, but in evil."

N'Djilékou answered, "Yes, it's all true. You hit the nail on the head! We should know how to build our present and secure better days for our children. Whoever you are, you will have enemies. Enemies do not lack and they will never lack; but we may miss our friends and we often miss them. So, let us not collect the devil's fruit to satisfy our selfishness and greed, and then jeopardize the future of our children."

N'Djilékou looked at the sky and realized that the sun was already down. The sun's rays were no longer scorching. N'Djilékou and his spouse got up and continued their journey. On the road, they kept on narrating past stories. They wanted to unload their bitter past on their road to Lafidougou. Lafidougou was not far anymore.

As they were walking, N'Djilékou saw Samba, the shepherd of Lafidougou. He was caring for his herd. Samba enjoyed cracking jokes. He was also well-known for his hard work. For Samba, idle time was the devil's time. That day, he was playing his flute as usual. A melodious sound broke the silent bushes. Samba moved and shook the bush and all its components. He was playing a song celebrating life in its complexity, life full of challenges and rewards. Everything was touched by the message. The atmosphere seemed to be suddenly thrilled. All the living particles seemed to rebel. They seemed to rebel against the world, against themselves, against this shocking, but true message, and even sometimes against God. Everything seemed to be moved and shaken by what existence and happiness may stand for, Happiness? Does it really exist on this Earth? Everyone is involved in a journey, but where does it take us?

Like N'Djilékou, everyone is after happiness on this Earth. Similar to Samba, everyone sings and cries, sometimes in search of happiness; a journey of hope, perhaps.

What a funny coincidence! N'Djilékou was going to search for refuge in Lafidougou and this young shepherd fed him with a great message.

Meanwhile, Samba's herd was grazing near the hill in the valley with a great pond and vast grassland. You could smell the scent of flowers, the green grass as the cattle was busy chewing, swallowing, and cutting, chasing insects by wagging their tails, blowing, and moving slowly. Flowers seemed to smile at the sky as a sign of gratefulness,

51

and as if to say, "Thanks be to God for having created us as flowers." Bees were also busily buzzing in search of their food. They also seemed to say, "Thanks be to God for creating flowers and for having created us as bees." Birds were flying and sometimes perching on the blossoming trees, singing melodious songs.

It was just marvelous and poetic. Everything seemed to travel. Birds were singing and hunting some unfortunate grasshoppers. All was full of life and struggle for life.

A little farther away, one could hear a strange hissing sound as if something were falling from the sky at high speed: *fuuuuuuuu.* A hawk was swooping down on a beautiful turtle dove. The turtle dove dodged the hawk and disappeared into the thick tree leaves; a narrow escape. On the horizon, another hawk was taking flight, circling around, scanning the earth below in search of a prey, or say, food. The unfortunate hawk, the one that just had failed to capture the turtledove, joined the other circling around. Both hawks then started to fight vigorously. What was the cause of their fight? Nobody could tell.

N'Djilékou sighed, "Oh yeah! Birds also fight. I can understand why animals often fight, but I cannot understand why humans, who claim to be intelligent, smart, also fight with violence. Why?"

"You make me laugh," Banko replied.

With a provocative smile, N'Djilékou asked, "So, what are you waiting for?"

Banko did not answer. She merely smiled back. As they kept walking, they got closer to Samba, the herder. When he saw them, he was a bit stunned. He recognized N'Djilékou because he used to come to Lafidougou on market days to buy or sell items. When he recognized them, he hurried towards them with joy and greeted them.

"Welcome, N'Djilékou! Welcome, Banko! How are you doing?" Samba asked smiling broadly.

"Thank you. We are well," N'Djilékou answered.

"How are the people of Tiala doing?"

"They are all well too. What about you?"

"We are doing well too." But he looked at N'Djilékou as if he wanted to find out more about N'Djilékou and his family.

"Yes, everything is fine. We'll see you in the village." N'Djilékou answered while waving good bye.

"See you soon," Samba said and then hurried towards a bull which was dragging behind the rest of the herd.

N'Djilékou and his family continued their trip to the village. A little later, they arrived in Lafidougou where the people warmly welcomed them. They went straight to the chief's compound. They found people at the main gate sitting under the shed. They greeted them in chorus. Then, the chief's junior wife welcomed them and took them to the guesthouse which was to be their temporary home. She offered them seats on a raphia mat and a traditional carved stool. Then, she gave them some fresh water. Later on, Wendé, the Chief came and greeted them and told them that his home was their home.

In Lafidougou, hospitality was the general rule. Their hospitality was well known in the four corners of the region. Cordiality and solidarity prevailed in Lafidougou. While chieftaincy was hereditary, it was still based on wisdom, experience, integrity and a strong sense of leadership. A true leader was the one capable of using the law to protect the people. The people of Lafidougou enjoyed their freedom, thanks to their good and open-minded leaders. N'Djilékou felt at ease among his new brothers and sisters.

They would organize the welcoming ceremony for N'Djilékou and his family. There would be dance parties. They would also organize the great counselling gathering and people would be given the opportunity to speak their minds, to share their wisdom and experience. Then, the newcomer would take the floor and all the audience would listen to him very carefully. At such gatherings, people were given the floor so that they might ask any question they wanted, but of course, wise questions. In Lafidougou, there were Muslims and traditional religion practitioners. Tolerance was central to their lives. Local residents lived together, shared views in harmony and brotherhood. Lafidougou was a peaceful village.

The Arrival: Celebrating Togetherness

Behind the huts, one could hear cows mooing. Samba was returning with his herd while playing his flute. He knew how to play music harmoniously. The melodious and captivating flute song floated in the air and plunged everyone into their dreams, giving the feeling of a long trip in the world of wonders. His music penetrated the soul and created the desire to know more about the complexity and perplexity of this world.

In the village, people were excited because a stranger had come to add something to their community. As the elders of Lafidougou used to say "communal and collective life requires open-mindedness." They were happy because they expected their "new brother and sister" to make their contribution to the development of the village.

As the elders used to say, "Collaboration is central in any growth process." In Lafidougou, sharing was central, not taking away or squandering. Giving and taking was encouraged. Looting, being stingy and stealing were condemned. The elders believed that "knowledge is like soup, and whosoever has it, should share it with the rest." It was against this background that the elders of Lafidougou used to organize counselling sessions where they discussed all the social and cultural aspects of life.

The muezzin started the call to prayer. From all sides, people were hurrying to make their ritual ablutions because God requires cleanness in prayers. Once they were done with their ablutions, they all rushed to the central mosque of the village.

On the horizon, clouds started to gather in the shape of mountains. From time to time, one could hear some distant rumbling announcing the arrival of the rain. Villagers were unhappy because it had not rained for a long in the area. Sacrifices and prayers had not helped. Plants began to wilt away. Nature became sad. People started wondering about the deep reason for this lack of rain. For some folks, the lack of rain was due to the murder of a young Mossi trader by outlaws. When such tragic events struck, people were left totally confused and the only solace they could find was praying and supporting each other. Often, small traders were the victims.

The villagers used to say that money brought all these types of murders to their communities. Long ago, they didn't know such useless and apparently gratuitous assassinations of innocent people. But the advent of money, cotton and the road changed the landscape and the relations among people. Cotton opened the thirst for money and the road opened the way for all kinds of bandits to roam the villages in search of victims. If you smelled money you were in trouble, they said. It was the curse of money.

In fact, it was said that the victim went to a neighboring village to sell his goods and when he was on his way back home, bloody thugs took away all his belongings and stabbed him to death. That bloodshed, they said, was the root cause of the lack of rain. The gods were angry and there was no rain any more. Today, the Muslims decided to pray and implore the sky for some rains. That was why they spent more time at the mosque than usual.

A cool wind was blowing. And some tree leaves were fluttering. Clouds began to spread and the sky became darker. Then it started pouring down. The sky seemed to be unloading its anger through terrible grumbling and lightening.

While it was raining, some women were busy finishing up cooking and washing their utensils. There was a pleasant smell in the air coming from the various compounds.

Some heads of families were telling stories to curious and inquisitive children. They gave children riddles, funny and yet very instructive stories. During such entertainment, some children dozed off, but others remained awake and kept on asking questions. After the stories, the children returned home to rest while waiting for the sun to break out. The elders used to say, "I'll put God's rope around the neck," meaning that they were going to sleep. When Moussa said so, the children around him laughed out loud.

"Papa, why put a rope around the neck? You're neither a goat nor a sheep," the children said.

"Oh! My children, you remind me of a funny story," Papa Moussa answered.

Demba, a curious boy, very keen on listening to elders, begged Papa Moussa to tell the story, "Please Papa, tell us this story. We want to know it. We want to learn more about it."

"Well, since you want to hear it, I'll tell you. In fact, once there was a fellow who was chatting with his friends. When came bedtime, his friends said, 'We are going to put God's rope around our neck.' This was a way to say that they were going to sleep. But, our fellow went into the sheep and goat barn, took the rope off of one goat and quickly put it around his own neck. When the morning came, the owner of the goats went to free his pets, but surprisingly enough, he found the fellow in the barn with the rope around the neck. He then asked him: 'Eh! What are you doing here with this rope around your neck? What are you doing in my goat barn?' Our poor fellow answered, 'what is wrong with you? Can't you see I've God's rope around my neck?' The goats' owner rolled with laughter. He laughed so loudly that all his neighbors came to find out what was happening to him. When they learned the reasons why the poor fellow was wearing the rope around his neck, they too couldn't stop laughing. Our fellow then became a subject of entertainment around the village.

"Oh! My children do not behave like this fellow. When our people say they are going to put God's rope around the neck, they mean they are going to sleep." The children enjoyed Papa Moussa's tale. After this story, they all went back to sleep.

The sky was getting darker. Insects were chirping. A short distance from the village, in the bushes, some owls were hooting. Children fear the hooting of this mysterious bird, which sometimes augured a bad omen, the elders used to say. According to popular beliefs, the cry of an owl near the village was a bad premonition. So, nobody wished to hear or to see it.

The night was opaque, a frightful opacity. During such opaque nights, people would not organize collective games or plays because they believed that it was risky to do so. At night, bad spirits roamed the country and they were likely to harm nighttime party-goers.

Tomorrow, the whole village would celebrate the coming of N'Djilékou among them. They would kill goats, sheep, and hens. They would also prepare a delicious *simu* – some juice made from millet flour mixed with water and honey. Various types of meals would be prepared for this special ceremony.

* * *
*

The rooster just sang: cock-a-doodle-doo. This imbroglio of cock-a-doodles announced that the day was about to break. A little later, the muezzin called out: *Allah Akbar! Allah Akbar! Allah Akbar!* From all corners, one could hear the slamming of doors and the noise of utensils. Men, women and children were going out for their daily chores. People started to get ready for the feast too.

On the horizon, the sun was coming up slowly. Behind the trees, it was slowly but surely moving up towards the other end of the world. It had just started its long voyage to feed its children with its magic and powerful light.

The tom-toms started to resound in the market place. From a distance, one could hear the drum rolling showing that there was a happy event unfolding. The shouts and handclaps of women thrilled the air. People were cheerful and they openly expressed their joy, either by dancing, singing or clapping their hands. Strong young men

63

were dancing energetically, jumping and trampling the ground. Young girls were dancing while moving their bodies like worms, just as if they were boneless, competing with the young boys who were capering about.

A group of women were busy cooking. Some children were jumping around and prancing out of joy. The tom-tom rhythm quickened. Some girls shouted out some *yuyu* to encourage actual or potential suitors. To motivate a good dancer, they would put some cloth around his neck. Sometimes, the women would bow down in front of the dancers while shouting out *yuyu* as a sign of encouragement and distinction.

With smiling faces, some elders were sitting under the shed and gazing at the youth capering and pirouetting with joy. N'Djilékou sat among them thoughtfully. "The people of Lafidougou are hospitable," he mumbled.

It was almost noon when the women started to serve the meal. Grouped by age and gender, people started eating. The dishes let off a very good smell in the air. People ate and drank with pleasure. The *simu* was abundant. Children had plenty to eat too. They even had trouble choosing which food to eat. Hands were landing in the dishes and people were sweating a lot. After this heavy meal, resting was necessary. No tree-climbing after meals, especially for children.

In Lafidougou, the local populations respect their customs, habits and the rules laid down for social peace. Laws were established to secure peace and order social. The word peace was commonly used in Lafidougou.

The feast continued. In the afternoon, people kept on dancing. On this special occasion, one of the notables would also deliver a speech on behalf of the Chief. This kind of address was meant to break the monotony. In the night, little children would sit around grandfathers and grandmothers. The elders would tell stories about the hare, monkey, hyena and many other animals. That was how wisdom and experience were transmitted in Lafidougou. Their grandfathers, the grandfathers of their grandfathers had also received their education in the same way. The storyteller was both amusing and instructive. Through these tales, children had fun and learned at the same time.

The tom-tom and drum beats began to slow. In the dancing arena, there was a cloud of dust. Young people, both old women and men were excited by the rhythm of the tom-toms. The sun was setting down and people began to return to their homes, either to rest or to complete their household duties.

From the bush near the village, Samba the shepherd could hear the harmonious and captivating rhythm of tom-toms. Samba walked slowly towards the village, with his herd. The dance was also nearing its end. Everything therefore became quieter and quieter. A captivating voice tore through the air and imposed itself on the crowd. It was that of the griot, the messenger.

"Eh! Eh! Eh! People of Lafidougou, open your ears and listen to this message on behalf of Wendé, the head of the village. As our ancestors used to say, 'All is well that ends well.' Before continuing what I have to share with you, I would like to remind you that this feast was organized to strengthen our relations with our neighbors. For all those who cherish freedom, solidarity and fraternity, we want to welcome and accommodate them among us. We have the duty and the full responsibility to strengthen our relations with such brothers and sisters. Our ancestors used to say that 'one finger cannot gather flour.' They also used to say that 'a single leaf cannot provide shade.' We need others to survive the bitter and unpredictable contours of life and existence. Brothers and sisters, fathers and mothers, sons and daughters, cousins and nieces, listen up!

"A person is not a person without others. To be a person, one must live among people. Yes, it is together, togetherness, hand in hand and with smile that we can build a harmonious society where human values are respected and cherished. Let us not forget, people of Lafidougou that, it is diversity that makes the beauty of this world. We therefore need everyone and everyone needs us. People of Lafidougou, as you know, salt alone cannot make good sauce. We need skills, knowledge and experience. So, we need everything and everyone to make this world and this community a better place to live. People of Lafidougou, to make a long story short, I give the floor to whoever wants to speak.

May God bless us! May God bless you all!" The crowd applauded with joy.

N'Djilékou took the floor and thanked his new village fellows, "People of Lafidougou, I thank you very much for your welcome and accommodation. Thank you all. I can't forget you. Yes, I will never forget you. May our relations be cemented and consolidated; I thank you from my heart of hearts. Only God will reward you for your good deeds. Dear brothers and sisters, I thank you and I wish you all the best." The crowd applauded loudly.

After the address, people started to scatter, to return to their respective homes. Silence invaded the dancing arena. As for Samba, he was busy leading back his herd to the stable. He was running left and right, trying to control the herd to get into the stable made up of thick and high wooden walls. This type of fence was meant to protect his herd against the attacks of lions and other wild beasts. When all was done, he returned to his house playing his flute. He rested a little and then took a bath. He enjoyed bathing with warm water, because warm water has no secret for him, he believed. He then enjoyed his food; some millet paste called *tô*, accompanied by well-seasoned okra sauce and guinea-fowl meat. When he finished eating, Samba thanked his wife who answered, "Thanks be to God." She then brought him his raphia mat to rest.

Samba spent the whole day running after his herd in a bush full of insects of all kinds. During this solitary walk, pitiless insects and small beasts bit him. From time to time, he would shout out loud to deter some stubborn cows from getting loose and running away from the herd. So many shouts and races after these pitiless and stubborn animals, so many insect bites exhausted Samba. And yet, he bravely faced the challenges. Samba liked to face up life with courage and wisdom. For him, "No one can gain their daily bread by being idle." He believed that it was necessary to work to avoid suffering or suffer for preferring idleness. He enjoyed hard work. Samba used to say that to be successful, working was not enough. What was really important and crucial was working wisely and smartly towards achieving one's goal and purpose in life. Samba always used to say that his own success depended on himself, self-reliance, and on the contribution and blessing of God and society.

Samba stretched out on the raphia mat with his face turned up towards the sky. He was busy admiring the stars, trying to count them. Some stars moved and disappeared into the fathomless pit of the sky. He was concentrated and deeply absorbed by his meditation, all the while thinking, "Did the stars kill the sun? Perhaps so! And yet, tomorrow, this very sun will reappear on the horizon. Does this imply that the sun is immortal? If it isn't the same sun that appears on the horizon every morning, then there might be infinity of suns. Perhaps so! Ah! I don't understand anything in this mysterious world. Why are we limited? Our ancestors said that long ago, the sun and the stars had fought. And until now, the war goes on. Oh God! But, why does this occur? In any event, God does not act at random. He knows what He does." Thus, Samba wondered about the complexity and perplexity of the world and did not find any solid and satisfactory response to his questions.

While Samba was busy in his chaotic meditation, Fatima walked towards him and asked, "Why are you so still?"

"What do you want me to do? Don't you know that I should rest after such a tiresome and hectic day? I spent the entire day running across the bush after the herd. So, I need to rest now."

"True! Well! Apparently today, you did not get any game at all, did you?"

"Ah! Thank you for reminding me. I have a hare and a hedgehog in my bag. I would be delighted if you could cook them tonight. Let me get it for you." Samba stood up quickly, then went to grab his bag and emptied the game in a basket.

"Ok, don't worry. I'll take care of that and in a little while you'll have them ready." Fatima assured him.

Fatima started cooking the game. She handled it very carefully and artfully. She was well known for her culinary skills. She had a moderate temper and never got discouraged quickly. Any time she came upon difficulties, she would find solace in these terms, "Insha'Allah, everything is going to be alright." Fatima was a great woman and

Samba always praised her culinary and social skills to other men, whenever he had the chance to do so.

The pot was boiling and singing a marvelous song as the meat was cooking. The vapor rose in the air in the form of a serpent and disappeared.

Samba was lying on his bed with his hands on his belly and his knees bent. He was enjoying the fresh air. During such times, Samba always took a deep rest and enjoyed every bit of it. He knew he should actually enjoy his rest at the moment because the following day, he would be back in the bush, running after his cattle.

The night was getting darker and darker. Crickets were chirping in melody. Samba wondered for a while and came back to his meditation. "Ah well, I don't understand anything in this world or at least I have a wrong understanding of things. Why so much suffering in this world? Ah, I see! Pride and ignorance mostly blind our vision. A proud person refuses to accept other people's suggestions because he sees tenderness and flexibility as a sign of weakness. And ignorance makes things even worse. By glancing at humans in general, I realize that they all act more or less the same way. For instance, some elders would say to a young person, 'You are very young and were born only yesterday. So what can you teach us? Where can you get good ideas and wisdom?' Ah! They forget that wisdom has nothing to do with age. There's no correlation between age and wisdom. They forget that a wise person can also be mistaken. In society, I noticed that whenever, someone raised his voice to say something, he would come under a barrage of attacks, just because critics wanted to show him that they knew him better than himself and that they knew what he wanted. But what is dramatic is that those people who claim to know everything are mostly ignorant and they don't even know that they are ignorant. That's the worst of it all.

"Arrogance is at the root of human suffering too. If only people could listen to each other very carefully and wisely, if only people could be humble and flexible, life would be better. But pride can destroy everything in us. Ah! I forget that we are limited. We cannot see beyond our limits. Our mind is limited. And it is because we are limited that we are proud. We personally refuse to recognize our weaknesses and thus generate hell in us and around us. We stand in our own way to peace and fulfillment. So, humans are very often the root cause of their own problems and pains. Yet they tend to blame their problems on Nature and others."

Fatima walked closer to him and asked, "Are you dreaming and speaking aloud? What's the matter with you?"

Surprised, Samba scrambled to answer, "Oh, no, I'm not dreaming aloud! Don't worry. Anyway, isn't it normal for me to dream out loud after such a tiresome day spent in the bush caring for the herd?"

"Well! But you shouldn't just start speaking out loudly while sleeping. It's not good. If you act like that, it should be for a good reason. Anyway, the meal is ready. Tomorrow, you may take it with you if you want."

Samba kept silent and did not answer. He was still dreaming. Fatima then persisted, "Oh! What are you thinking about exactly? You worry me too much."

"Well! Samba sighed. "Since you are curious about what I'm thinking, let me tell you then. I would like to know why humans suffer."

"It's very simple. God divided the world into two parts. There is the day and there is the night, heat and cold, there is fire and there is water. When it is hot, you think of cold. So when you are happy, you also think about misfortune. "You want everything, here and now. And that's why you suffer. So, to avoid suffering you must set a limit to your desires and wants. When your wants are limited, you'll suffer less. When you break the limits of your body and mind, you go insane and sick. Both body and mind should work harmoniously to keep things in balance." Fatima argued.

"That's sounds a bit true. But…"

"But what?" Fatima emphasized, "I repeat; you should see the world as it is and not as you want it to be by all means. Stop living in your imagination. You may re-arrange things in your mind, but that won't change the order of things. It is useless to complicate your life by trying to understand everything in this world. Well! You know; I'm sleepy, I should go to bed now. There, I will be at peace instead of torturing my brain for nothing."

"You find that useless?"

"Don't you know that your questions will not change the order of things? I don't know; perhaps they can relieve you. In any case, I think your meditation is useless and fruitless because it won't take you anywhere but to torture your peace of mind. You'd better do other things than torture yourself. The world is simple and I just can't understand why you keep teasing out your brain with such things."

"You are starting it again. Please, stop it!"

"Well! You started it. No?"

"Ok, you are right." Samba finally admitted.

Then, Fatima went to bed in her beautiful and quiet mud-built house which represented a real paradise for her.

At the entrance, there was an average sized terrace and on the left, a traditional grinding stone to crush millet and other cereals. Just above the door, she hung some corn which was dangling tied together with a tree fiber. Further inside the house, she placed earthenware, jars, baskets, water-pots and a wooden case. The large earthen jars contained peanuts mixed with some ashes. Fatima did this to protect her grains against harmful insects. In the baskets, she put dried beans and baobab leaves. The wooden case contained her loincloths, bracelets and jewelry. Each time, after her housework, she carefully collected her kitchen utensils and placed them in a special wooden box that she had bought at the local market. When the roof of the house leaked, she hastened to repair it very carefully and artistically.

She often used to say that "only personal efforts are fruitful and rewarding." She wasn't a foul-mouthed person who would spend the day cursing around and treading on others. She was instead a person of principle, kind and reserved. She always preferred actions to words. That was the reason Samba had always loved and cherished her. Fatima was the woman of his dreams. He used to say that he couldn't find any better. "Take Fatima from me and my whole life falls apart," Samba always used to say.

The night was getting darker. Toads were singing in the nearby water ponds. From time to time, the steps and noise of people walking in the night interrupted the melodious croaking. The voluptuous and captivating songs filled up the air, giving the impression of an orchestra. The sharp chirps of crickets also broke the opaque night and sometimes disturbed the sleep of people in the neighborhood. A child screamed out and a scolding voice of an adult, probably her mother, could be heard. A dog barked out loudly. Everything was a combination of rhythm of all kinds, consolation and complaints.

Suddenly, an earsplitting noise tore through the sky, over and over again and died down. That was the wizard bird! Any time that it flew over an area making such a terrible scream, which was said to foreshadow misfortune, the women clapped their hands; marabous recited some verses from the Quran to fend off the evil spirit. Such actions prevented the evil from reaching vulnerable children, they believed. Unfortunately, if children fell sick because of these disastrous cries, they could easily die. Few healers could fight this evil. And the most gifted ones made a great deal of fortune out of this shameful trade. They were pitiless. To cure any benign disease, they used complex ceremonies that required fortunes. They resorted to the ancestors through sacrifices and prayers, the supreme divinity, and evoked the name of all the spirits. Their charge was at least a calabash full of cowries, a black goat and a white rooster. Some people paid anyway, as health has no price. So, they accepted self-sacrifice to recover their health. Such were the practices which had developed in the villages surrounding Lafidougou.

The prevailing order was an accumulation of fortune at the detriment of care for the neighbors. Money had destroyed everything and hypocrisy became the most predominant attitude. People got lost in the midst of all this hypocrisy and material-centered world. Money took over humanity. Everything was money, nothing but money! Easy money and fortune took over common sense. Greed, nothing but greed, greed only! Instant gratification became prevalent. Confusion and rush for fortune were in people's minds. Greed created a real storm and turmoil. Society was suffering under the rule of money. Money has no humanity, even though it is made by humans!

For instance, last year, in Tiala, Tinga's wife died of malaria. Truly, Tinga did not have enough financial and material means to fend for his family. After a hard fight, after spending all that he could spend to save his beloved, Tinga was penniless. Then the race for assistance started. Tinga ran everywhere, but couldn't come up with anything promising. Everywhere he went, he was clearly told that there was nothing that could be done to help him out. Discouraged, weakened in his heart and soul, he was totally devastated, hopeless, helpless and lost. "Bah! What to do next? To fight or not to fight; No way!" he wondered. He then decided to see his uncle Banlè who was among the richest in the village. He rushed to his house. When he got there, some kids were playing and having fun in front of the compound. He asked them about Banlè. The children quickly accompanied him in the yard and returned to continue their games, which interested them more than anything else at the moment. "Wow, these children are well-behaved indeed!" Tinga said.

A few moments later, Banlè appeared. He was walking heavily like an elephant. He had a mighty belly and a thick neck, which clearly showed that he was living in a mint. He had such a huge belly that he was moving like a pregnant woman expecting quadruplets. Some villagers used to call him the king of ugliness. He offered Tinga some water to drink as prescribed by tradition and then asked the reason of his visit, which Tinga quickly explained.

With a haughty voice, Banlè went on to ask, "But since when am I your uncle? Huh? Tell me. And besides, I cannot spend my wealth on you! I have many other things to do with my fortune rather than waste it on stupidities."

Calmly, while thinking that he who begs shouldn't be ashamed, Tinga added, "Uncle Banlè, please try to understand my situation, my wife's life is in danger. I am in real trouble. I am in a very desperate situation... And I need... I mean..."

Banlè thundered, "Stop your nonsense! Who doesn't have problems? Huh? Tell me. Everyone has problems. And I do not want to see your face in my house again because you are a man with problems. I am not here to solve other people's problems. So, understand that I can't do

81

anything for you. You better get out of my house now!" Completely lost and feeling abandoned, Tinga did not know what to do and where to go. He had done everything he could do. He went almost crazy and was about to throw himself on the ground and cry like a child. He did not know who else could help him out. Then, it clearly dawned on him; he understood that he couldn't save his loved one. He was probably going to lose her.

Tinga then decided to go back home. He lost hope in life and humans. He traveled through the entire village; however, nothing good came out of his race. Nothing good! He was only rewarded by failure and the refusal of those who could afford to provide for assistance. He began to doubt about humanity. Can humans really help humans? He wondered. He staggered under the effect of deep disappointment and discouragement. He was living his own hell already on earth among his fellow beings or at least in a hell created by his fellows. As the popular saying had it in those days "those who live or deserve to live are those who have the means to buy health and to prolong their lives." That was too costly for him. When he got home, he found his love in a critical situation. She got weaker and weaker and was struggling for her last breath. She fought all alone against death. Tinga burst into tears. He was just there watching his wife struggling and being taken away by death. He could do nothing. It did not rain. It poured. Tinga ran to his wife's aunt. When she saw him in such a desperate mood, she started quivering out of fear. She began bombarding him with lots of questions? Tinga was more confused. She followed him back to his house and when they got there, she realized the extent of the damage.

"Oh my daughter, don't you give up the fight! Hold on tight Louti!" Her aunt desperately implored her.

There was no answer. A few minutes later, Louti asked for some water to drink. With some extra efforts, she managed to swallow a few drops. And then all of a sudden, her head dropped backward. She passed away. Sadness and sorrow thus fell heavily on Tinga's shoulders. He couldn't do anything to prevent this from happening. As the ancestors used to put it, "What must happen, will happen. There is no way to prevent what the gods planned." The worst happened to Tinga. Louti left for good.

Such is life. The earth keeps on moving while millions of Loutis are packing up for an endless journey. She left, never to return. She joined her ancestors.

Poverty kills in silence. Such is the world. Louti left. Millions of similar souls will know the same fate as Louti. They will all travel with no hope of return because there is no return.

A voice whispered in his mind. Just travel in this world and learn the lesson. Just travel. The voice kept on repeating the same words. Travel and learn. Travel and learn! Travel and learn! Travel and learn!

Banambonon's Marriage

Seven years after their settlement in
Lafidougou, Samba's cousin, Gorko asked
Banambonon's hands in marriage. Gorko met
Banambonon during one of his regular visits to his
cousin Samba. One day, as he was sitting in front of
the compound, talking to his friends and cousin,
Banambonon passed by on her way to fetch water
from the common well. She greeted them and went
on her way. Gorko was struck by her beauty and
grace. He quickly asked Samba whether she already
had a suitor. Samba replied that in fact a couple of
suitors had asked her for marriage, but they were
turned down as Banambonon did not like them nor
did her parents. Gorko was excited to give it a try,
and yet, he was concerned that he might be turned

down too. His heart started pounding at high speed. He became silent for a while. Then, he said, "I would love to be her husband and I would do everything under the sky to be her husband." Gorko therefore decided to send his relatives to express his interest for Banambonon.

N'Djilékou welcomed the request and was happy about it. However, he wanted to make sure that Gorko was responsible, respectful and reliable. He wanted to ensure that his daughter didn't fall in the hands of an irresponsible and immature husband. So, when Gorko sent elders from Sanfodougou, a neighboring village, to ask for Banambonon's hands, N'Djilékou's response was that he heard them, and that he would talk to his brothers and sisters about the request. He already knew Gorko's family. He discussed the matter with Banko, and then, did his little investigation about Gorko. He quickly found out that Gorko was a caring human being. He could be a reliable and responsible husband, he concluded.

For N'Djilékou, marriage was not a private affair. It was a family affair. It was about love, honor and respect. He loved his daughter so much that he didn't want anyone to play around with her.

As required by his tradition, you don't approve a marriage request immediately when someone requests your daughter for marriage. Also, you don't refuse bluntly if someone asks your daughter for marriage. There were various forms of marriage in his society: love-based marriage, arranged marriage also called *lusi*, which literally means receiving a woman, and leviracy. Unless someone was well-known for his immaturity and irresponsibility in the village, blunt rejection of marriage request was rare.

When Gorko sent again his friends and relatives to find out about the status of his request, N'Djilékou told them that the road was cleared. Gorko knew that he had to bring a hen, also called *kolo-mundo*, which means "rolled up chicken" in a new calabash. So, Gorko killed a hen, plucked it and then removed the intestines. He gave the *kolo-mundo* into a new calabash during the *muntolo*, which is the harvest feast. Gorko's close friend brought the *kolo-mundo* gift to N'Djilékou who approved it.

That was an initial gift to show his willingness, and the fact that he was serious about his request.

Marriage gift giving always followed the same tradition. *Muntolo* was the period of harvest, joy and blessing. It was the time of gratefulness and reciprocity. *Muntolo* was the time to thank the gods, spirits, ancestors and *Labara-Nkondo*, that is God on High. It was therefore the appropriate time of sharing and gift-giving. Marriage gifts such as *Kolo-mundo* were offered at such times to request the blessing of ancestors, the gods and spirits.

Kolo-mundo was one of the steps of the bride price followed by *djo-djiyan,* which is the mobilization of the groom's relatives and friends to work on the in-laws' farm. Gorko's friends also went to till Banambonon's peanut farm. When the *muntolo* feast was over, Gorko waited a couple of months and sent the *taguma-paa* or formalities price, which amounted to 1000 cowries paid as part of the bride price. A year later, when Banambonon was eighteen years old, Gorko sent another bride price: one hen and one rooster to complete the bride price payment process. That step corresponds to the blessing stage, which brings more luck and blessing to Banambonon. It is also called *mèwara,* which literally means massaging the body to keep away bad luck and evils from undermining the woman's reproductive capacity. According to tradition, violating that stage and having intimate relations could undermine the woman's reproductive capacity or it may even bring her bad luck.

When all the formalities were completed then came the moment of truth for the wedding ceremony.

The wedding occurred after the harvests. Before the wedding, Gorko sent his friends and relatives to inform N'Djilékou's family about their plans to organize the wedding ceremony. Being a Muslim, Gorko decided to go the Muslim way. However, N'Djilékou decided to consult a local diviner to ensure that the ceremony occurred smoothly without any incident. Banambonon's aunts, cousins, nieces, friends and uncles came from Lafidougou to attend her wedding and support her.

Also, all the women in the neighborhood mobilized to prepare the bride. During the preparation, Banambonon was secluded. During that period, neither Gorko nor any other man was authorized to see her. Only women took care of all the preparations, including food preparation, plaiting Banambonon's hair and putting *djabi* (also known as henna) on her feet and hands. The day of the wedding was her day, and everybody ensured that she enjoyed it to the fullest. The ceremony started on a *kari*, which is Sunday. On *alamissa*, which is Thursday, they brought her out of the house and her husband took her home.

Young girls were singing, and blocking the way to prevent Gorko's friends and brothers to reach Banambonon. That was a very important step because each side had to show its determination to keep the bride. Gorko's group had to hand over more cowries to negotiate their way out. The struggle, the bargaining and negotiation went on until late into the night. Finally, Gorko's group was able to sneak away with Banambonon to Sanfodougou which became her new home.

Banambonon's marriage was a source of joy and hope for N'Djilékou and his family. Banko was also proud that life was getting better for her and for her children.

A year later, Banambonon was blessed with her first child. She called him Abdu. He was named after Gorko's great-grand farther who was well-known for his bravery, wisdom and honesty. He used to own six hundred cows and hundreds of goats and sheep. When Banko and N'Djilékou got the news about their first grand-son, they were more than excited. They paid Banambonon a visit and took part in the naming ceremony.

According to their tradition, you only give a name to the child at the *yimbo* ceremony, that is, the naming ceremony or head shaving ceremony, which occurs a week after the birth. It is only after the naming ceremony that the child acquires a personhood in society. There was no ceremony before that day. Abdu's naming ceremony was a great feast. It was the opportunity to thank the gods, ancestors and *Labara-Nkondo* or God on High. N'Djilékou offered him a cow, a ram and a sheep as a reward. Banko brought three very nicely made clothes and a blanket. People came from

Tiala, N'Djilékou's native village and from Lafidougou as well to participate in this great event.

After this happy event, came Banambonon's first ordeal in handling the baby. She had difficulties breastfeeding Abdu who was a cry-baby. She was very confused and did not get any rest, especially at nights. A month later, she decided to return to Lafidougou to her parents' for some assistance.

Her mother, Banko, helped her a lot. She would take care of the baby while Banambonon was sleeping. Banambonon spent one month there, and the situation improved. She learned to handle the baby by herself, to wash him using the appropriate potion made from local plants. The plant-based potion was meant to strengthen the baby and also to keep away bad eyes and evil spirits.

On each market day, which occurred every three days, Gorko would pay them a visit. He would come to the local market to sell some leather, hens and a couple of sheep and goats. He would seize such opportunities to spend quality time with Banambonon and the baby.

As Banambonon became more skilled and savvier at handling a newborn baby, she decided to return home. A month later, she returned to Sanfodougou to live with her husband who was excited to see them back.

A couple of days later, he decided to celebrate their return. He organized a small feast and invited his relatives and close friends, including Samba to join him in the celebration. Samba opened the event by pouring water on the floor three times followed by blessings and prayers.

At the end of the feast, Samba blessed again the baby and his family as follows, "may God bless the baby and his parents. May Abdu be a child that will make you proud. May he carry the torch and make our people proud. May he grow to help you grow older and happier. May Abdu crawl, stand up, walk and be our guide."

Your Farm is Our Farm

Years after Banambonon's marriage,
N'Djilékou and his family were living peacefully in
Lafidougou. His daughter Banambonon got blessed
with a healthy baby. N'Djilékou also was blessed
with two boys: Gontan and Pèret. He was well
respected in the village. He built beautiful houses
and had many goats, sheep, cattle, horses and
donkeys. Many people were impressed by his
fortune which kept on growing. He thus held a
significant place within the community. A man's
place in Lafidougou was based on how hard
working he was and not on where he came from.

He cultivated a vast farm and each season,
young people in the village would come to cultivate
it. They would spend a whole day working on

94

N'Djilékou's farm and he rewarded their labor accordingly. Each one received either some money or a basket of millet.

Indeed, collective farm work was very common in Lafidougou, and it could take different forms. It could be in the form of *kudjèma* which means, helping one another, in other words mutual work. *Kudjèma* is usually built on friendship and kinship relations. Friends or relatives would come together to set up their *kudjèma*. It could extend throughout a whole month, and during the various phases of farming activities, namely clearing, planting, weeding, and harvesting. For the most part, *kudjèma* occurs during the weeding or cultivating phase. On a rotating basis, members work on a given member's farm. Then, they take turn until all members' farms are cultivated. During such work, the person who receives the groups on their farm cooks delicious food, and serves his colleagues with some *yii* (traditional beer made from sorghum) or *simu* (millet flour mixed with water and honey). The head of *kudjèma* or the workers' manager is called *tiéla*. He or she is the mediator. Should there be a conflict at any time or any cancelling of a specific farm work, the *tiéla* informs other members and chooses another day as it fits. *Kudjèma* is not just about working together. It is based on the philosophy of being there for others. It develops a sense of community and togetherness. When a mishap occurs to one of the workers, the other members support him or her. *Kudjèma* helps them consolidate bonds; it builds group ethics and a social support system in a community whose livelihood is mainly based on farming. *Kudjèma* is mostly done by men, but women could also engage in it. Whether organized by men or women, *kudjèma's* principle and philosophy remains the same.

In Lafidougou, Tiala and other surrounding villages, *kudjèma* was indeed a very common farming practice. Money was not really the motivator of such solidarity and collective work. It was rather motivated by a good sense of solidarity inherited from their ancestors.

There were multiple forms of community support mechanisms during the farming season. Community solidarity was especially popular during the rainy season. Sometimes, an entire neighborhood would go and farm for someone who provided support to the group such as paying their taxes for them. As they have a great deal of respect for their ancestors and traditions, each generation would pass onto the next, these values that keep the whole community together in times of joy and pain. There was a kind of implicit contract so that every rainy season, the youth of the village went to work on N'Djilékou's farm.

Finally, the special day arrived. That day, some clouds were accumulated at the horizon. A fresh wind was blowing which moved the leaves of trees. As the sun started rising up, the youngsters rushed towards the farm accompanied by the rhythm of tom-toms and drum beats. They shouted, jumped up and down, expressing their joy. Some were testing their hoes to ensure they were sound and operational. When the youth got to the farm, the rhythm of tom-toms and drums accelerated. From far away, one could hear women's *yuyu* chants encouraging the youth. Everyone wanted to show their talents, because it was during such occasions that people liked to be distinguished for their prowess and talents. Work was what gave a person a privileged place and social status within their community.

When the youth arrived on the farm, they quickly lined up on its edge. The rhythm of tom-toms rhymed beautifully with the creaking sound of the *kana*. This unison of rhythm was known as *kambô*. *Kambô* is a farming method during which cultivators made alternating noise with their hoes while tilling. The alternating noise of hoes creates a harmonious rhythm. The rhythm is always accompanied by captivating songs and the beats of tom-toms. The workers would skillfully till the wet soil.

N'Djilékou was following them. He was lifting up some of the young plants that got covered by the tilled soil. The joyous shouts expressed by the women thrilled the air, thus creating a mixture of captivating rhythm, an unprecedented rhythm. As to the old men and women, they could not cultivate at the same rhythm and with the same vigor as the youth. So, they were in a different group. Sometimes, they would shout out "Haya! Haya! Go ahead! Go ahead! Courage! Courage!" They were shouting so, as a way of encouraging the youth to keep on farming harder. The workers were sweating as if they were soaked by the rain. Their sweat was a clear sign of their devotion and hard work. Among the young, Lamouni and Djikouma were well known for their skills in handling the traditional hoe called *kana*. From sunrise to sunset, they worked hard, and the griot kept on praising them.

Kanama, the flutist, played a melodious and voluptuous song. He was well-known in the village for his skills. The tom-toms and drum beats rhymed with the fluting. No words could really capture that melody. It was just beautiful and attractive. The rhythm drove people to finish cultivating the entire farm.

The sun began to shine stronger and stronger. It was already in the middle of the sky when the women brought some food for the workers. There were about ten baskets filled with food accompanied by delicious sauce and meat. As usual, the women invited the workers to come to eat.

Banko went to N'Djilékou and told him that the meal was ready and that he might invite workers to eat. N'Djilékou therefore addressed the workers as follows: "Dear brothers and sisters, you are invited to join the shade," which means to eat. But Doro, the *tiéla* or the workers' manager, replied that they were going to finish farming a remaining small portion before eating. Everybody had to listen to Doro because the *tiéla*.

After cultivating that piece of land, they split up in different groups. Young people sat in a different corner, under a *néré* tree, that is, the African locust bean tree. As for elders, they were gathered under a wild grape tree. Women gathered under a shea-tree. The grouping under different trees had nothing to do with the species of the tree. It was just done at random. Once people grouped as expected, they started eating. One could hear tongues clicking, giving the impression of an orchestra. As people were all busy eating, all of a sudden, a sharp noise tore through the air.

In fact, two dogs were also having their meal. They began disputing over a bone and it ended up into a biting session. One of them was called Toura, a massive dog with extraordinarily sharp canines bit Kaba, a medium-size dog, in order to snatch the bone. But Toura did not intimidate Kaba; so the fight intensified. They were quickly separated and the bone was given to a different dog that devoured it at once. Justice was done. Neither Toura nor Kaba got the bone.

After eating, the workers rested for a while to facilitate digestion. While they were resting under the trees, some of them were chatting to while away the time. Some spoke about their adventures and others of news that had been reported to them. Lamouni and Djikouma were sitting under the compact shea tree, and they struck up an extremely curious conversation.

Lamouni cleared his throat, tapped Djikouma on the shoulders, and asked, "Boy! Did you hear by chance the failed assassination of Manlè last time? And you know what! This was done through the complicity of his own brother, Dji?"

Djikouma stared at him with eyes his wide-open, "Pardon me! Go ahead! What?"

"You are not in the news. I can see it."

"Ah yes! But which Manlè are you talking about exactly?"

"Manlè, Gnessa's son of course." Djikouma emphasized.

"Gnessa's son?"

"Of course!" Lamouni stressed, and then repeated, "The son of Gnessa indeed! You know, Manlè was going to visit his farm. And by a fortunate coincidence, he dropped by Tialo's traditional beer bar. He went there to drop his five liter bottle and when returning home, he would stop by and collect it. That was when Tialo grabbed him by the hand claiming she had something serious to tell him. So, he followed her around the corner. And then she sold out the secret. She told him all about the plot."

"Eh! Was she informed about the plot?"

"Yes! She got news about the plot."

"And how did she know that?"

"I don't know how! But she was informed. Tialo thus exposed the problem to Manlè who returned home and took his shotgun with him, loaded it, then went to his farm. He put his bike under a tree, then climbed in a quite leafy tree and awaited his antagonists patiently."

"Han! What an audacity! And what happened then?"

"And then, a little later, he heard strange noises. It was the voice of his potential murderers, walking slowly on dead leaves, armed with machetes, heavy sticks; they went carefully under the tree while throwing from time to time some quick glances to make sure nobody was coming. It was as if they were hunting and on the lookout for their prey. Manlè watched them carefully while they were moving towards the tree where he took refuge. As a former veteran, he controlled himself, and kept quiet. The whole situation reminded him of a battlefield where strategy, surprise and swiftness mattered a lot. So, he stayed calm, took all precautions to avoid being detected because the worst could happen if his enemies were to find him. Some pitiless ants pricked him, but he bit his lips to overcome the pain, because the least noise could draw the attention of his hunters, or at least of his potential murderers. Then, they stopped right under the tree in which he was hiding. He was able to identify all of them. However, his brother Dji was not among his potential murderers."

"But where was he, this imbecile?"

"I don't know anything about that. But, he was not among them."

"Didn't he shoot them?"

"No! But he shot just beside them. And they all took to their heels! They scattered in the bush like panicked guinea fowls. Each ran shouting and screaming for their lives. One of them even urinated on the spot. In fact, they were much surprised. And you know well that surprise can kill! They had a narrow escape from death and they screamed loud enough to break their vocal cords."

"God was just with him. But why his blood brother, same father and same mother wanted to take his life?"

"It was just because of his pension! And yet Manlè never forgot him each time that he took his pension. The ungrateful and selfish dirt bag wanted all the money. He wanted it all."

"Eh! Money! It will make many people insane. It is the incarnation of the devil. And it is money that ruins our world. Today, my dear friend, money replaced fraternity. Ah! What a shame!"

"Ah yes! It is the shame of shames; shame for him to want to kill his own brother because of money."

The conversation stopped there because the work had to resume. Doro's voice came out loudly: "Stand up! Stand up! The sun will set down soon." All the workers stood up at once and began to work. The beat of tom-toms and drums resumed and filled the air again. The women started their shouts of encouragement *yuyu... yuyu.... yuyu...* The hoes made some creaky noise as they came into contact with the soil, "*rack... rack... rack,*" tilling portions of the wet soil. The grasses collapsed in the process. In front of the workers, grasshoppers and other insects fled. Unfortunately, some frogs got their legs hurt by the sharp-edge of hoes. They cawed out in pain. Sometimes, the noise they made was pitiful, but the workers completely absorbed by their labor, couldn't pay attention to such complaints.

The portion that remained should not take more than half an hour. The youngsters were tilling enthusiastically and sweating a lot. The rhythm of tom-toms changed at once, switching to a rhythm that expressed bravery and victory. Suddenly, a victory shout filled the air, *"yaa... yaa! yaa... yaa! yaa... yaa!"* The *tiéla* announced that they had finished cultivating that farm! Other workers shouted in chorus with him, *"Baaba yaa! Baaba yaa! Baaba yaa!"*

The workers then decided to go onto another farm located approximately a kilometer from the one that they had just finished farming. Some ran, while others walked there. On arrival, they started to farm immediately without wasting time.

In the sky, swallows were flying and diving while making sharp screams. And very far away, some birds, vultures and crows were performing gliding flight. According to folktales, up there in the blue sky, these vultures and crows used to organize their festivals with the gods.

But down on earth, on the farm, everyone played with joy and exuberance. Despite their age and physical weakness, the elders were very engaged as well. They also worked hard. Sometimes, to encourage the youth and to accelerate the work pace, the elderly women sang captivating and voluptuous songs that even motivated workers to work harder. Such songs were inspiring and they were meant to encourage workers to challenge themselves.

Everything was both rhythmic and melody. The *kana* started to creak loudly, "rack... rack... rack," which announced once again that they had finished cultivating that second farm. A victory shout once more filled the air.

N'Djilékou then thanked them for their effort and hard work: "You worked well. May God reward you; may He compensate you for your great support. May you go back in peace and happiness! May you live as long as you want in good health and happiness! Our elders used to say, 'A single leaf cannot provide shade.' What you just achieved justifies the veracity of this proverb. But brothers and sisters, I'll make it short. Once again, I thank you from the bottom of my heart for your great achievement." Doro, the workers' manager added: "Don't worry; your farm is our farm. Our ancestors used to say that working together is what makes the soul of our tradition and values."

The beat of tom-toms and handclaps mixed with the *yuyu* of the old women thrilled the air. In the end, the workers returned to the village with joy and pride. As for N'Djilékou, he was smiling broadly, which clearly expressed his total satisfaction.

That year, rains fell abundantly and the harvests were fruitful. N'Djilékou was blessed with a great harvest. He built two additional barns to keep his harvest. He began to forget his past sorrows and the suffering inflicted upon him and his people by cotton, the road and the dam. Lafidougou was indeed a land of peace and prosperity for N'Djilékou who always praised his ancestors and the gods for blessing him and his family.

It Came Like Lightening from the Sky

Years went by, and N'Djilékou and his family lived happily in Lafidougou. Gotan was approximately eleven years old and Pèret nine. The family atmosphere was pleasant and filled with love. Such was life in N'Djilékou's family.

One day, in the middle of the night, N'Djilékou woke up shaking. He screamed so loud that he woke up Banko, his wife. It was a bad dream; a real nightmare. He dreamt that a boa attacked his goat and started swallowing it. He surprised it and hit it right on the head. It spit out the goat and turned against N'Djilékou. The boa bit him on his right hand, and swiftly wrapped itself around his legs and threw him against the wall with such violence that the wall shook. It started to squeeze his legs and the saliva was all over him. His right hand was bleeding profusely. He was panting, searching for something to hit it with; then, he screamed for help. There was nobody around to help. Fortunately, there was his old hoe around, he stretched out his left hand and grabbed it, and then hit the boa hard on the head repeatedly. It unfolded and freed him, and then slipped back into the darkness. N'Djilékou screamed loud for help once again, only to realize that it was a bad dream. So when Banko woke up, N'Djilékou was shaking and sweating profusely. The following day, they decided to consult the oracle to find out exactly the meaning of the dream. The oracle told him that he had to perform sacrifices because the gods said he neglected to share his success by refusing to partake in the *muntolo*, the harvest feast. Yet, N'Djilékou had sent to Tiala all the required items for *muntolo*, but his brother Touko had kept them for himself and never performed any *muntolo's* requirements on N'Djilékou's behalf. He sold them and bought some traditional beer instead.

A couple of months later, the dream came back in a different shape. It materialized. This time,

N'Djilékou surprised a real boa slipping into his bedroom in plain daylight. He screamed for help, and then rushed to grab it by the tail and pulled it. The tail was very hot and burned his palm. Neighbors came to his rescue and helped him kill the boa. N'Djilékou understood that there was something really going on. The boa embodied his ancestors' spirit. It was their totem. He therefore understood that there was something afoot. But he didn't know exactly what it was all about. He consulted the diviner once again. However, even the diviner, the great Doko, couldn't figure it out. He was asked to sacrifice three goats and a ram. Because the boa spit out the goat in the dream, it wanted to take actual revenge. It wanted its goats by all means. N'Djilékou fell sick for a whole week. He had a real high temperature and a severe headache. Banko consulted several traditional healers who gave her all kinds of potions and plants. N'Djilékou eventually recovered and became himself again. From time to time, he would go visit his farm. Life went back to take its normal course.

Then, came the day; a day that marked a turning point in N'Djilékou's family. That day,

N'Djilékou decided to go visit his farm. But how did such an unpredictable and fatal event happen? No one could have predicted it. It moved like a lightening from the sky and altered once and for all the course of N'Djilékou's family life and existence. But nothing can stop destiny from happening.

When N'Djilékou arrived on his farm, he made a tour of the entire farm. He found that all was beautiful. His farm was very green. As he was admiring the plants, he felt something awkward in his body, something chilling. He was getting weaker and weaker. He felt as if his heart were squeezing and burning. As he grew dizzy, he decided to sit down on his hoe. He was still able to sit on the hoe. Then, he froze. It was too late. He had just gone.

This was the sudden and fatal event that plunged N'Djilékou's family into a total panic and utter loss. Banko couldn't understand and might not understand this sudden and unexplainable death. She became a widow overnight.

The day of the tragedy, Banko and the children were home. She waited and waited impatiently for his return. She did not know what had happened to him on the farm. Tired of waiting, she decided to join him on the farm, just to see what was going on. When she got there, she shouted and called out his name "N'Djilékou!" Again, there was no answer. Then, she became more concerned. She continued to run across the farm calling him. Again, there was no answer. Far away, she saw a human shape in a sitting posture. "Maybe that's N'Djilékou sitting there," she said. Banko got closer to him and asked him what he was doing in that position. Again, there was no answer. He was calm, quiet and almost motionless. She came along, grabbed him by the shoulders, shook him and stepped back. He fell down from the hoe. At that specific moment, she saw the fate awaiting her: a widow, she had become. "He died! He died!" Panicked to death, bewildered, she couldn't understand what was going on. She was completely lost. She could not know what to do next. Her existence had become empty. Banko started shaking in the face of the irrevocable. She wished she could disappear at once, and penetrate the soil. She was lost and very confused. She had no raison d'être any more. She wanted to die too. But then what will the children become? Finally, she decided to return to the village.

She started to run. She ran, stopped sometimes, and ran again and again, panting with pain and confusion. She staggered and was breathless. She only felt sorrow and confusion. Her legs were wobbly and heavy. Existence and life became empty and meaningless. The whole universe seemed to ask her: "Why are you crying? Why are you running so madly? Why do you stagger like that? Why? Why?" It was an event beyond her control and understanding. Bad luck struck her. She felt victim to the hazards of life and existence. In the loneliness of her misfortune, Banko was choking. She was struggling hopelessly to catch some air. Her world turned upside down; a total chaos. Then, questions started boggling her mind. "What will I become? What about the children, who will help me take care of them and educate them? Who?"

Finally, she arrived in the village and went straight to the house of the village chief to announce the awful news. Without wasting time, the chief sent young people and his personal healer to the farm to check the situation. When, they got there, the healer touched N'Djilékou, pressed his wrist, bit his toe and shook him. Then, he performed some rituals, poured some water on the ground while calling on the spirits, the gods and ancestors. However, N'Djilékou didn't respond. The healer concluded that he was gone. So, they put N'Djilékou's body on a horse-driven cart and rode back to the village.

As N'Djilékou's death was confirmed, the chief decided to send someone down to Tiala to inform his relatives. In no time, the messenger got there and most people were informed and they quickly got ready to do something. The pain was general. "It is not N'Djilékou that died, but rather Banko," the Head of the village said. N'Djilékou's relatives mobilized and went to Lafidougou as soon as possible. Even though Lafidougou was his new home, since his relatives required to bury him among his ancestors, Lafidougou chief didn't object to the decision. They would accompany the body to his native village. Together, they would organize the burial and subsequent funerals. When N'Djilékou's relatives arrived in Lafidougou, everything was ready. It only remained to depart with the body to Tiala. In Lafidougou as in Tiala, sadness was general.

The chief sent a messenger to inform Banambonon about the sad the tragic loss. When she got the news, she was totally brokenhearted and inconsolable. She threw herself on the ground and begged the gods and ancestors to bring her father back. Gorko tried to console her, but he too was devastated by the news. Friends and neighbors came to support them. Finally, Gorko and Banambonon decided to go to Tiala. When they got there, they found that the atmosphere was tense and full of dirge. It was a mishap to the entire village. Some flutists were playing funeral music too, which even exacerbated the situation. However, tradition required such music because it was believed to help overcome the pain and tragedy associated with death.

In the central house, women got together and cried in unison. Their faces expressed deep sorrow and disappointment, especially for a premature death like that of N'Djilékou. Some women tried to contain the pain that was eroding their souls. But sometimes, they could not hold it for long and burst out in tears again. That was the scenario at the heart of the central house. As the women were weeping, the funeral music kept coming on.

That day Samba, the shepherd, remained home. He could not go to the bush to look after his herd. He stayed with the children and comforted them. His fellow shepherd took care of his herd. As for his wife, Fatima, she was with Banko. Fatima kept on repeating to her that "misfortune happens to everyone." But nothing in the world could prevent Banko from weeping. The event exceeded what she could take in. She loved N'Djilékou. Yet he passed away without even leaving a message. All this eroded her and drew her pain even worse. She cried, but her tears wouldn't come out any more. The pain reddened her eyes. "If only he had said something to me before dying that would have perhaps comforted me. But, he left without saying anything to me. He is gone forever. Gone forever! Oh my God! Oh my God! I will not see him anymore, never again." Such were the words that were coming out of her mouth every now and then.

So, when everything was completed, the head of Lafidougou gave the permission to take the body to Tiala. The body was accompanied by cries and beats of tom-toms. Banko and the children left at the same time as the procession for the native village, Tiala. Gonta and Pèret were on horseback. They were completely lost. Their single angel left them down in a world without mercy. When they arrived in the village, the body was placed in an area called *djirimbatiè* or the "place of the dead." Everything was carried out according to tradition and beliefs. Nothing was left to chance.

The sun was setting down and the clouds became redder instead. The entire village was quiet. One could only hear the cries, the beat of the funeral tom-toms and the sad melody of flutes. A little later, the beats of tom-toms changed. Abruptly, the women started a funeral dirge.

Some ran towards the cemeteries while screaming, others sang in a shaky voice. They were carrying in their hands a piece of straw to accompany the body to his last destination. Elders poured water on the soil. It was the water that the deceased was supposed to drink before undertaking his long journey to the hereafter. So, when they got to the cemetery, they processed around the tomb three times without stopping. Then, they put the body beside the grave. They wetted the soil to build a small wall that would prevent the soil from reaching the body. After these rites, they buried the body. Then, they returned home. Women were screaming but the men were walking silently. From time to time, you could hear some of them clearing their throats and sighing.

No smile in N'Djilékou's family. So much pain was eating away at their hearts. They could not digest this terrible loss. Banko was still weeping.

On the third day, they organized the *laason* ceremony. That day, they prepared beans, peanuts, cooked leaves and killed a goat. This was called *laason*. The ceremony would be attended by the soul of the deceased person, the elders said so. The soul acted completely the opposite of what living humans do. According to elders, diviners could not take part in those ceremonies, because when they saw the actions of the soul, they would get nausea. The soul of the deceased person ate in a disgusting manner, they said. It chewed food and put it back in the dish, which was disgusting.

After that ceremony, on the tenth day the *lulaynis*, that is, the aunts and sisters of a deceased person would leave the common compound. Their departure puts an end to the funerals. The *lulaynis* should not cry any more. But Banko continued to cry. Ten days of sobbing, ten days of heavy sorrows, ten days of melancholy. When the *lulaynis* left, Banko really felt the emptiness around her. The world became unbearable. Existence became meaningless for her. Nobody seemed to hear her cries or feel her pain.

The only person that was supposed to help did not show any signs of help. That person was Touko, N'Djilékou's brother. Touko wasn't even worried at all. He was rather busy collecting N'Djilékou's belongings and properties. As the saying goes, "Evil does not ask for an appointment. It just knocks at your door." N'Djilékou's premature death took Banko by surprise. Tragedy knocked at her door and there was nobody to lean on. She was left to herself with the two children.

One day, N'Djilékou appeared in her dream and told her that she should not worry. He told her that he was in a better place and that he would take everything to protect his family. He instructed her to perform some sacrifices by offering a goat and a ram to the gods. Banko informed Touko about N'Djilékou's request, but he dismissed it. So, she took things in her own hands and performed the sacrifices.

The Orphan Wipes His Own Tears

Touko, N'Djilékou's senior brother, was a man with a stony heart, a self-centered person whose only concern was to drink traditional beer and merry. He had no compassion at all for Banko and her children. Touko had collected the entire heritage and had sold everything. Touko, Bèrè (his wife) and Saaga (his son) embodied real evil. They plundered the heritage to the detriment of Banko and her children. They came to Lafidougou, collected all the millet and sold it at a cheap price for traditional beer called *dolo* and to have fun. N'Djilékou's death was a source of party for them. Saaga was a "spoiled child." He stole everything and his parents refused to punish him. They simply forgot the proverb that has it that "spare the rod and spoil the child."

Months went by. Years after years, the situation of Banko and her children worsened. Finally, Banko decided to remarry. Her new husband was Djibo. Gontan and Pèret stayed at Touko's house. Touko did not do anything else other than to mistreat them. Gontan and Pèret did not know anymore where to go. They did not have enough to eat any longer. Overcome by the suffering, they decided to run away and to join their sister, Banambonon, still living in Sanfodougou. Banambonon had also suffered much from the cruel loss of their father. Night and day, she too was concerned with the future of her two brothers. When the two children arrived in Sanfodougou, they were cordially accommodated. They spent a year and half with their sister and lived a really happy life.

Over time, Gorko, their sister's husband started to find their presence unbearable. He did not want to see them anymore in his family. He therefore pushed for their departure telling them that he had married their sister but not them. He gave them some millet, some clothes and asked them to leave.

Banambonon tried to persuade her husband to keep them, but without success. He had become too obnoxious with no regard to his wife's opinion. So, he refused categorically to listen to his wife. He wanted the children's departure and nothing more. And if Banambonon persisted in defending them, she could join them in their journey.

The universe seemed to turn upside down for them. N'Djilékou used to tell them that in life bad things often happened to good people. "Sometimes, the world would crumble around you for no clear reason. Every good action you did would lead to negative results instead. You may never understand why. However, you should keep doing the right thing, no matter what." N'Djilékou used to say.

Indeed, Gontan and Pèret went through all kinds of ordeals after their father's death. They could not enjoy their childhood to the fullest. They were embarked on a seemingly endless journey. An apparent endless journey filled with ups and downs.

However, they did not despair. They still hoped and hoped for the better back to Tiala.

In the morning, with the first songs of roosters, the two children got ready for Tiala. On their way, they kept meditating on their fate. "What is held in store for them in this journey in search of peace and love in this crazy world? Should they return to Lafidougou or Tiala? No! Return to Tiala to live with their mother." They finally settled for living with their mother in Tiala.

When they arrived in Tiala, they went to Djibo's house. Nobody was there to welcome them. Sheep and goats were lying under the shade of the barns, busy ruminating. On the cracked wall, a redhead lizard was nodding as a sign of welcome. There was nobody in the house. Their mother had gone to the farm. As for Djibo, he had traveled to a nearby village. The two children rested under the shed. They were worried because they did not know what Djibo would say. Would he accept to accommodate them? What about their mother, what will she say or think when she sees them? She wasn't expecting them. They entrusted their fate in God's hands.

A few moments later, they saw a woman carrying on her head a bundle of wood. As the woman got nearer and nearer, they recognized her. It was their mother. Her neck shortened under the weight of the load on her head and she was sweating abundantly. When she recognized her children, she smiled. The two children also smiled back.

She dropped her load and walked towards them saying, "My lovely children, come and give me a big hug! It's been so long. Have you drunk any water?"

Gontan replied, "No Mommy, when we arrived, there was nobody home."

"Come, my children. Get yourself some fresh water to drink."

"But Mommy, you also need to drink water." Gonta answered.

"True my children. When I saw you, my heart started dancing. Come. Follow me under the veranda. There, we'll feel much relax and talk the way we want."

Banko brought out some food, reheated it and then served them. After enjoying the food, the conversation went on.

Tapping Gonta's back and while holding Pèret's hand, Banko exclaimed, "Wow! You grew up so quickly in Sanfodougou! My children, your absence made me suffer a great deal. Don't you see how I lost weight? This was the result of sorrows that eroded slowly my soul and spirit. God saved me my children and I thank Him. Your arrival is almost a miraculous cure of my sorrows that stifled my soul and sucked my blood."

Pèret said smiling, "Mommy, we are very glad to see you again. We will stay from now on by your sides. Together, we will rebuild our lives."

"Ah! What a great idea! But tell me! How is your sister Banambonon?"

"She's doing great. She's even expectant." Gontan answered.

"Great! Thanks be to God. What about her husband?" Banko asked.

"Fine too." Both Gonta and Pèret replied. Then, Gonta added, "by the way our sister's son, Abdu is also fine and he is growing fast."

"But you didn't tell me why you came so unexpectedly. So, why are you here? Is it your sister who sent you back here? Tell me what brought you here." Banko asked emphatically.

Gontan quickly replied, "Mommy, you are right to ask these questions. We returned because our sister's husband didn't want us around anymore. He ordered us to leave. We had become a burden for him. So, he asked us to leave his house."

With deep disappointment in her voice, Banko asked, "Really! I am shocked. Did you hurt him by any chance?"

"Never ever! As far as we know, there was no problem." Gonta replied more emphatically.

Still in shock, Banko persisted, "Did he quarrel with your sister?"

"No." Both children answered. Then, Pèret added, "Banambonon never quarreled with him. We are not aware of any misunderstanding between them. Really, we do not know about an argument between our sister and her husband."

"Anyway, Insha'Allah, everything is going to be fine," Banko said while tapping their backs. "As your father used to say, 'keep doing the right thing, no matter what.' This man is ungrateful! But he will bitterly regret it one day. He will learn that life is not selfishness, but rather solidarity and mutual support. I have always had great respect for him and he had never shown any sign of irresponsibility at all. However, he showed me his real face without any detours. He was carrying a mask and time unmasked him! He should be ashamed of himself. Yes, if he is conscious and responsible, he should be ashamed of his deeds. You can't kick out orphans just like that. But, unfortunately men of his kinds are unconscious and irresponsible."

As if to console their mother, Gontan said, "I don't know. But as the saying goes, time allows humans to contradict themselves. What he did, will go away. Yes, it will go away because everything goes away in this world, except Allah."

Banko paused, and said in a soft and lovely voice, "My angels please listen carefully to what I have to say. You are from now on at Djibo's house, my husband. He will treat you as his sons and you must treat him as your father. Be nice, my children. Be polite and respectful. Respect comes before everything. It is the most basic rule of life. Never be rude, obnoxious or lazy. Be hard workers and responsible. Then, we'll all be happy. When Djibo is back, I will tell him why you are here. Together, let us face life with optimism. Do you understand what I mean?"

Gontan nodded, and then asked, "Mommy, when will he return?"

"He will return this evening. Don't be discouraged or stressed for nothing because you are from now on at home with me, beside your mother. I'm here to protect you. Allah will not leave us in shame. My children, you are a remedy for me. Before your arrival, let me say that again; I took refuge in my dreams to drown my sorrows. Allah can do anything and everything. I did not know that I would see you so soon. Well, I think you need to rest now. Alright, I'll go fetch some water at the well so that you can take a bath. You should clean now. After bathing, you will feel much better."

Gontan replied while smiling, "Mommy, we are not as tired as you believe it. We will go with you to the well. You need our help, don't you?"

Pèret confirmed, "True, Mommy. We'll go with you to the well."

"My angels, you must rest. Fetching water is the work of adults." Banko said smiling.

Gontan scratched his head and responded, "Mommy, you may be right, but that does not prevent us from helping you. We are now grown-ups and we can fetch water for you. Don't worry Mommy."

Banko finally agreed, shrugged and said, "Okay, since you're insisting, so come with me. Take a bucket. I will take the basin."

The two children went to the well to fetch some water. They went back and forth and filled the two huge earthenware jars. Afterwards, they washed themselves and changed their clothes, then took a rest.

*
* * *

* * *
*

A couple of hours later, Djibo returned
home. He was carrying a bag on his head and a
leather bag on his shoulder. Gontan and Pèret went
to meet him and welcomed him. They took his
leather bag. Djibo then went to rest under the
veranda. Banko brought him some fresh water to
drink.

His friend Larba, who lived in the
neighboring village, had invited him to a child-
naming ceremony. The arrival of a newborn was
regarded as a feast. Djibo's friendship with Larba
stemmed from the fact that he had lent Larba a
piece of land. According to tradition, one does not
just give land to anybody because land is sacred and
belongs to the ancestors. Anyone acting against
traditional land management and distribution rules
was severely punished. Djibo was well aware of this
and he chose to give the plot of land to Larba

because he had rendered him a great deal of good services, including paying his taxes.

When Djibo finished taking his bath, Banko explained to him why the children came home. He smiled, and then answered, "They are also my children. No, I don't have any objection. But what will their uncle Touko say? Won't he be bothered by the presence of the children at my house?"

Banko countered, "No, I don't think so. I don't think so. He should rather be ashamed for not being responsible enough to help raise his late brother's children. Remember the kids were under his custody and the only thing he was able to do was to starve them. They fell sick and he did not even care about them. Instead, he was busy plundering what their father left as heritage. Remember that the kids suffered from guinea worm and couldn't walk at all. Touko refused to feed them. His wife prepared food and refused to serve them. She gave them millet flour and asked them to cook by themselves. As Gontan and Pèret couldn't move properly, they left the flour untouched. So, each time that Touko and his family returned from their farm, his wife would say, "they are not even hungry, these wizards! If they were hungry, they would have cooked." Bèrè pushed her husband to mistreat the kids. She was really bad. Sometimes, their aunt Nado prepared food for them. Touko's wife couldn't accept that. So, they would even go to Nado's and dared beat her for giving food to the children. Given all their deeds, I don't really think he'll dare come and say anything about the kids. Anyway, when the kids left and went to live with their sister Banambonon, where was he? What did he do? Nothing! He thought that by acting so brutally towards the kids, they would die. But, Allah is great and we thank Him night and day for His help. Our ancestors used to say that a witch lays egg when she cannot harm your soul. Touko laid his own egg; the evil part inside him came out. He revealed his true face. Allah is great. Shame on him!"

While fondling his beard, Djibo said, "Hum! Life is not a problem, it is problem-solving. Problems are the spice of life. They make it sweet and bitter. Suffering is a learning process; it is part of life. That's why it is often said that after the rain, the sun shines. Who could have imagined that my father could become the richest of this village? He is originally from Sampara.

But how did he find himself in Tiala? Well! I'll tell you how. Long ago, the White men came in our land with cannons and shot people who refused to submit to their will. Then, the head of the white men came to Sampara with an interpreter and another white man. The purpose of their visit was to annex the village, but the head of the village refused categorically. It was known that after refusing to submit to the white man, he would come with his men and destroy the whole village. So, the young people got organized and mobilized to face him up and fight for their freedom and beliefs. Each fighter was armed with machetes, clubs, spears and poisoned arrows. The young people sang war songs while leaving the village to fight their invaders. But the white men had "fire sticks," that is, guns" which killed remotely. The white men's God thundered; that was how the guns were called. Each thundering was accompanied by the fall of about hundreds of people. All those who fell did not rise again. The people saw that they could not withstand their enemies. They panicked and scattered in the bush crying in despair. My father ran away. He scratched himself and was hurt everywhere; he was bleeding all over. Fear took over and he did not even feel the pain. He then arrived in Tiala and settled here. He did not have any material property, except the breeches he was wearing. But today, he has many goats, sheep, donkeys, horses and cattle. He has about thirty barns. He experienced misery and suffering. Finally, he became rich and happy. That's life."

Djibo spoke while gesticulating to draw the attention of his listeners on the importance of the subject. From time to time, he would remove his colorful bonnet to scratch his head. He was wearing a dress patched together. His leather shoes were in front of him during all this talk. His face was scarred all the way down to his chin, which is a sign of identity in his society.

He scraped his throat and said calmly, "misery can knock on everybody's door. It visits you without notice. There is always in the life of a man, moments of distress. Events crop up from nowhere and destroy your existence. But, my children let me tell that you need to fight to make it in life. Quitters never win and winners never quit. Never attempt to do evil in your life. Yes, it's true that life isn't always fair. The best aren't always the winners. That's something you may never understand. However, always seek to understand, even those who are radically opposed to you; because it is through open-mindedness and flexibility that you will understand this world and your kinds. The truth is that you will only begin to be happy when you open up to others and accept life as it is. My children, you must learn to love and to be tolerant in life. Do not be like those people who always curse society and everybody when they face a problem. Don't be like that at all. Be responsible for what you do and what you say. You will be real men when you know and accept this basic truth of life. Work hard and you will see that the sun will shine on you and for you. Do not be afraid of labor! Work the land and don't be afraid of being dirty because working the land will help keep your dignity clean. I tell you my children that a man without dignity is a man with no value or future."

After his long speech, Djibo stood up and went towards his leather bag. He asked his wife to bring him a basin, which she quickly did. He therefore emptied the contents of his leather bag in the basin. It was roasted meat. The kids were sitting quietly and watching him. In such situations, it was not recommended to show impatience or one's weakness for meat. That could be interpreted as a sign of lack of self-control or bad education. Gontan and Pèret were very calm, and even ignored what was happening around them. They still remembered N'Djilékou whipping them for failing to control themselves in front of smoked meat. Kids were not allowed to pounce on meat or any food that wasn't for them. N'Djilékou admonished them and told them that their greed would kill them one day. When a child could not control his greed, the elders used to say his intestines would move out and graze one day.

Djibo sharpened his knife against a stone and started to cut the meat in small pieces. He asked Gontan to help him, which he promptly did. Then, he shared the meat and the kids ate with satisfaction.

Djibo took his father's share and gave it to him. He just briefed him that he would like to talk to him about something really important. His father acquiesced and Djibo returned to his seat.

As there was not a lot meat, he did not share it with the entire extended family. Tradition recommends that food be shared among family members and failing to do so was a sign of selfishness, of being stingy. A person that eats without thinking of his father and mother is not respected at all in the community.

As it was getting darker, Banko was busy accelerating her food preparation in the kitchen. The smoke made her choke from time to time.

Tomorrow, Djibo will inform his father about the presence of the kids in his house. Knowing him, he was quite confident that his father would welcome the idea of taking care of the kids.

In the morning, Djibo went to greet his father as usual and took that opportunity to inform him about the presence of his wife's two children. He explained in details the reasons why the children came to his house. His father found that his attitude was full of wisdom. He seized the opportunity to stress that in life, one should never reject children under any circumstance. For him, children are the future of humanity. They are like angels. They make the world a beautiful place to live in. According to traditions, bearing children brings more manpower. It was seen as an honor to one's ancestors and a blessing from the gods. Children of other members of the community were also considered as everybody's children. Djibo's father, therefore, concluded that Gontan and Pèret were his own grand-children.

Then, Gontan and Pèret went to greet Djibo's father who received them warmly and considered them as his grandsons. He took the opportunity to advise Gontan and Pèret to be wise and to act with intelligence and respect. He reminded them of the conditions under which he had come to Tiala. He had arrived to Tiala almost naked. But, thanks to God, he was today living well and he did not have any problems at all. He was well accepted and integrated in his new community. He restarted a new and prosperous life. "Whosoever you are in this world, you define who you are and what you are. Sometimes, you can be your own enemy in the pursuit of your dreams. Don't stand in your own way. Don't be your own enemies. In life, it is vital to forgive, listen, understand, cultivate tolerance and love," he added.

Both children nodded and thanked him for his words of wisdom and for embracing them as part of his family. Djibo's father believed that self-fulfillment was achieved through connecting to others, being self-reliant and extending oneself beyond one's little world.

Coming of Age and Being Self-Reliant

Months went by and the two children were enjoying life in Djibo's house. The rainy season was approaching and they were enthusiastic and ready to go to work and start a new life.

First, they went to the farm to clear it and to spread out some fertilizers to enrich the land. This was the period for preparing farms and getting ready for sowing and cultivating. It was the hardest part of the year. During those moments, the sun was blistering. But the courage and goodwill of the peasant farmers enabled them to bear the blistering sun. The elders used to say that to be a real man, overcoming pain, especially bearing the sweltering sun was necessary. So, together with the children, Banko also brought manure for the fertilization of her farm. They were working hard in preparation for the rainy season.

However, one morning, when Banko woke, she felt a pain in her ankle. She couldn't understand what was going on. The pain was similar to an insect bite. When she checked carefully, she realized that she was suffering from the beginning of "guinea worm." "What a disaster! Who would work on my farm?" she wondered. The disease could take several months before being completely healed. If she did not find an effective remedy, she might suffer for a long time, which could harm her farm work. While she was in her bed and could not walk, Gontan and Pèret worked hard on her farm.

Djibo didn't waste time. He consulted different traditional healers to treat the disease. They traveled to the surrounding villages to seek the most efficient remedy. Luckily, they found the right medicine and cured the disease.

That year, the rain fell heavily. Thanks to the children's efforts and courage, Banko's farm turned green with marvelous plants. Passers-by admired the work carried out by her two brave children.

Gontan and Pèret also had their own farm. Each day, they rose early in the morning and went to cultivate it. They worked hard and finished weeding it. They helped Djibo to cultivate his big farm, which was also the collective farm. The rains were abundant and plants were green. Happy harvests were very promising.

Gontan and Pèret grew up quickly. They became more mature than expected. They took their destiny in their own hands despite the hurdles of life. Their good harvests impressed their fellow villagers. The inhabitants of Tiala were astonished to see these two young men growing richer and richer. They would say that Gontan and Pèret got their fortune from shamans. Others held that their prosperity was the result of their hard work. Gontan and Pèret decided to build a huge barn in which they put their harvests.

Djibo also built another barn on top of the others that he already owned. The family was happy. The children started to forget their suffering gradually. They decided to build a house. And they did it successfully, thanks to the good collaboration of friends and cousins, because the construction of a house was always done collectively. It was the sign of solidarity in the community. "Everybody needs everybody to make progress in this life," they said. And the people understood and set up a social system that guides and enables them to fight and resist unforeseen forces and evils of the dark.

Years went by and Gontan, Pèret and their mother lived in peace at Djibo's house. Gontan and Pèret were now involved in small trade in the village. They sold smoked fish and kola nut. They decided to spread out their wings and fly by themselves. In the village market, they often faced harsh competitors. But, they were always victorious. They learned to fight and they also learned to win. Their goods were of good quality and they sold them at truly competitive prices. Gontan bought a bicycle for his stepfather, Djibo, and another one for himself.

Life became very promising. They now planned to travel the world to learn more and to enhance their understanding and develop their business. Gontan used to bike to the neighboring villages to sell his goods. As for Pèret, he sold the rest of the products in the village.

Gontan married Sè and had a handsome little baby boy called Tchiri. The young couple was happy. The sun of their success began to shine brightly. Gontan and Pèret learned how to overcome various challenges. Touko, who hated them and endeavored to create a real hell for them, used to ask them for assistance. His family was living in misery. They could no longer fend for themselves. Saaga, their son, had become a dreadful delinquent and a threat to his own parents. As the saying goes, he who sows the wind gathers the tempest.

Gontan had a secret project. He wanted to leave the village and travel the world to broaden his horizon and understanding. But, he wanted to wait until his brother Pèret got married before taking off for the exploration of the world. Such was the idea that was crossing his mind for months. He wanted to go to Felikro, a neighboring country, where rains were abounding and manual labor was well compensated. He would be working in the cocoa and coffee plantations to improve his life and future.

But his wife, Sè, was a little concerned. So, one day when Gontan talked about it with her, she just said, "Well! My darling, you know I am not against your trip to Felikro, but what about us, I mean Tchiri and me? What will we do?" Gontan would answer that since he did not know much about Felikro, it would not be safe to bring all his family members there. He wanted to travel and explore the area and find out if he could cope with it before they could join him. Sè never objected to the idea. She just wanted to make sure that once he left them behind, he wouldn't forget them as some youngsters used to do. Departing for a foreign country could be a source of divorce in a couple's life. She knew that situation and that was the main reason why she kept on insisting that once in Felikro, Gontan should do all his best to come back for them. She didn't want to stay alone in the village. Gontan would pray and ask for God's blessing and protection because life in Felikro was said to be very tough.

As time went by, Gontan was always preoccupied with the idea of leaving his village, his country and going elsewhere in search of happiness, hope and healthier life. He could recall a lot of stories of fortune and misfortune for all those who preceded him in this adventure. He knew that emigrating has a lot of implications.

Nobody knows what such adventure holds in store. For instance, Gouli, one of his friends, went to Felikro. He spent five years there and could not even send a penny to his parents to support them. People used to say in the village that he became a highway bandit and was killed like a dog. All this created a great deal of worries and pressure for Gontan. He still remembered the case of his own father who emigrated to Lafidougou and ended it tragically. So, why emigrate if one can make it at home among one's family and friends? He knew that when you travel to another place, you have to learn their way of life, their language and understand their customs and beliefs to better integrate in that society. So, why try to embrace the unknown when his life had started to prosper in his own village and among his people? But then, he would say that to be a man, one has to accept the unpredictable and face up the unforeseen sides of life. His brother Pèret did not like the idea of adventure so much. He found life in the village very prosperous and he could not understand Gontan's determination to travel. He always tried to avoid any conversation or topics relating to his brother's future plans.

So, when Gontan informed their mother about his plans, she replied that he should be patient and wait another year. She would pray and make sacrifices and beg the ancestors and spirits to facilitate and protect him in his trip to Felikro. Any time Gontan talked about his trip plans to his mother, she would always respond in those words: "We'll look into it my son. We'll look into it when the time comes. You don't travel like that. You have to look into it before. So, be patient. I am working on it." She knew that Gontan was strongly determined to travel and she did not want to hurt him, nor make too much ado about it because this could even attract bad omen on her son, she believed. As for Djibo, he was also informed about Gontan's plans, but did not object. He only blessed him and told him to be patient and added that at the convenient moment, everything would happen smoothly.

As part of his preparation, Gontan decided to renew his national identity card. He knew he had to go to Felikro but he did not know in which part of Felikro he had to go. Every time he thought about his trip, he would remember what happened to his late friend Gouli and also the corrupt police officers who would not hesitate to plunder emigrants on the road. They were supposed to protect them and enforce the law, but corruption and the greed for easy money became so powerful among the police and customs officers that they would always take more than the transportation fees. When a police officer asked for your papers and you produced them, he would slap you hard to intimidate you. Then he would take your identity card and require money before giving it back. Such were the hardships that adventurers faced on their way to Felikro. There was no pity or respect for human dignity in some places. They were determined to empty the pockets of the poor immigrants in order to get enriched in no time. 'So, why emigrate to such a country where you will mainly suffer whereas at home you feel comfortable and happy?' Well! Gontan thought that going abroad would allow him to enhance his understanding of the world and to create new opportunities for him, just like Koro, who came back three years ago and built concrete and corrugated iron houses in the village. Koro now owned his own shop, as well as hundreds of cows, sheep and goats. He became a model of success and emulation for the youth in the village. So, given Koro's prosperous situation, Gontan did not despair because he believed Felikro could be a source of more prosperity and happiness for him too. So, he too just wanted to give it a try.

On the Road

A year later, as planned, Gontan decided to go to Felikro. He packed up his luggage and went to the local bus station. That day, Pèret accompanied him to the station. As for Sè, she was reluctant to go with him to the bus station, but in the end, Djibo and Banko persuaded her to go. So, she left Tchiri home as he was sleeping and went with them. Djibo and Banko stayed home. Banko blessed Gontan before he left the compound and emphasized that once in Felikro, he should not forget those he left behind. She said, "I trust you and I am confident that you will make it. Just rely on Allah and nothing bad will happen to you my son." These words echoed in his mind as he was standing at the bus station waiting. Around eleven at night, the bus to Felikro arrived. It was packed with other young people from the neighboring villages. They were all heading to Felikro in search of hope and prosperity. The apprentice shouted out "Felikro! Felikro! Felikro! Felikro!" meaning that the bus was heading to Felikro. So, Gontan greeted Pèret with his left hand as requested by tradition, which holds that whenever traveling one should greet with the left hand. He did exactly the same with Sè. Doing so brings fortune and blessing to the traveler. Gontan, Sè and Pèret were all on the verge of crying because the separation was very hard to bear. But they had to separate. They got a grip on themselves and did not burst out in tears. And Pèret said, "I wish you good luck and do not forget to send us a mail once in a while when you arrive at your final destination. Keep us informed about your situation. May Allah bless you." Sè kissed him and whispered in his ears "I love you." As they were exchanging farewells, the apprentice shouted out again: "Hurry up! Hurry up!"

Gontan got on the bus and sat beside an old man of about sixty years. He had a gray beard and was smiling broadly and looked like a happy man. The old man moved a bit to allow for more space and Gontan sat down. "You are welcome," he said before adding, "So, are you going to Felikro?" Gontan just replied with a short and breathless "Yah." It was as if he had just got rid of a heavy load. Gontan wasn't in a mood to talk. The bus started to leave slowly. Pèret and Sè waved their hands to say good-bye.

The old man asked, "You look a little worried my son!"

Gontan answered in an attempt to cut the conversation short, "No! I am fine. I am just tired and a bit sleepy."

But the old man went on to introduce himself, "My name is Salif and I have been living in Felikro for about twenty-five years now."

Gontan then replied, "I am Gontan. Wow! Twenty-five years!"

Salif asked, "So, where in Felikro are you going?"

"I am going to join my friends in Morikro." Gontan answered.

"Oh! Really! I am in Morikro. I can't believe we are heading to the same destination! And who are your friends?"

"I am going to join Lamouni and Sibiri."

"Well! Lamouni and Sibiri are both contractual workers in my coffee and cocoa plantations. Lamouni decided to leave after the harvest. I may need someone to replace him. And I would be more than happy to have you replace him if you want."

"Oh! Thank you very much. I was really concerned because I did not know what I would be doing there and how I would get a job. Thanks God I met you!"

As they were busy talking, the bus driver stopped all of a sudden. Some police officers signaled and ordered the driver to stop at the checkpoint. They asked for identity cards. The apprentice requested each of the passengers to pay five hundreds CFA Francs "to buy the road," which meant corrupting the police officers. If they didn't give money, they would be uselessly required to spend the night there for no reason. This could delay their trip and add more to their suffering. All the passengers were already aware of the police officers' expectations, so they did not dispute the apprentice's request. "What a world!" Gontan said. And Salif, the old man, added that corrupting police and custom officers on the road was part of the ordeal that emigrants to Felikro were accustomed to.

"In fact, whenever the police arrested you and asked you to speak a *proper language*, they meant you have to give money. If you failed to understand their language, you might end up in trouble, whether such as by receiving a hard slap on the face or being pulled out from the rest of the passengers, knocked hard and kept in jail until you paid the money. Corruption became part of their habit and daily behavior and discourse. Every traveler to Felikro knew that and was psychologically and morally prepared to abide by their rules. The local authorities and the respective governments did not care about what was happening at their borders as long as their power was not threatened. To avoid trouble, people became cynical and even encouraged the police and customs officers to misbehave. Sometimes, the police and customs officers would not even open their mouths to ask for money, but the drivers and their apprentices would request money from passengers in order to buy the road, as they used to put it. Such was the norm. You know what? The old man continued. Last year, as I was coming back from Felikro to see my parents in the village, the police officers in Felikro who were even worse than our own local police officers hurt a young man who tried to resist against them. He told them the law should protect the people and not the opposite. I still remember his words, "Anybody that oppresses people and traumatizes them in the name of the law is a criminal." He called it "abuse of power." They could not tolerate that challenge. He refused to pay the money and the police officers pulled him down from the bus and bludgeoned and bloodied him because he dared challenge their authority in front of the other passengers. He was crazy enough to challenge them. Nobody dared challenge them, my son! Later, I learned that the victimized young man was a law student and he was traveling back home to spend summer break with his parents. He got hurt for nothing. They blamed him for speaking big French and for trying to teach them what justice meant. When the law becomes oppressive, it muzzles the people. It is the end of reasonable speech. He said he was going to take them to court, but I don't know whether he succeeded in doing it. The court itself is corrupt through and through. So, my son, don't put your life at risk for nothing by challenging them. Give them the small amount of money they are requesting and they will leave you in peace. If you try to challenge their law-based decisions, you will always be told that nobody questions nor seeks to understand what the law does to people. We all know that the law alone cannot hurt people. It is the law enforcers who abuse their power."

Gontan was silent and completely disheartened by the old man's story. He was speechless.

"You see," the old man went on, "during the days of the white man's rule, we used to pay taxes and we were forced to work for free. We thought that with the white man leaving our homeland and giving power to our own brothers, we would live in peace and happiness. That did not happen at all. Our own brothers turned against us and started looting and cheating us. But we can't fight because they have power, guns and the law on their side. Only a fool will dare challenge someone holding a gun! As the saying goes, the toad doesn't dance with the hens or else it loses its eyes."

Gontan nodded in acquiescence, "Yes, the toad doesn't dance with the hens. That's true. If you have a gun in your hand, you can do anything you want."

"That shouldn't be the case! If you don't have a gun, use your mind as a gun to reason the one with the gun, because he who has a gun does not always have a sound mind! So, on this road to Felikro, use your mind to win over the gun owners." Salif countered.

"True indeed!" Gonta nodded.

Gontan was tired and sleepy. He started yawning and Salif understood and said, "My son, I think I'll let you sleep a little. We still have a long way to go."

On their left, a young couple was sitting with a newborn baby on the mother's lap. The father was snoring with his head slightly leaned towards his wife who would push him from time to time to get rid of his weight. As for Gontan, he was trying to find a comfortable position to sleep.

He noticed that Salif's head started to tilt. Everybody was sleepy.

The bus drove for about seven hours and reached the last city of Ganda-Gulo, located at about ten kilometers from the border. It stopped for passengers' identity checks by the police officers.

The border city called Nyamadougou is multicultural and very lively. People from different socio-cultural backgrounds lived there. It was also known as the city of no virtue as every kind of evil was committed including holdups, rapes, manslaughter and prostitution. It was the favorite meeting place of highway bandits who did not hesitate to attack travelers. Whenever travelers reached Nyamadougou, they moved together in small groups to avoid being attacked. The local police officers never cared about the crimes taking place around them. When they were called for rescue, they would always come several hours after the criminals had vacated the crime scene. If people happened to arrest a bandit and bring him to the police station or to the gendarmes, they would see him on the street the following day. The police and gendarmes were in league with criminals. This was how the city came to be the most infamous of the country. The local people were no longer at ease and stopped bringing bandits to the police to seek justice. Street justice took over. They developed the habit of rendering their own justice by killing bandits and thieves. Sometimes, when a criminal was arrested, he would beg people to take him to the police station, as he knew that once there, he would be freed in no time. There was no real security at the border. Protracted and entrenched violence became established in the area. The only thing that the police and customs officers were able to do was to plunder travelers.

As the bus stopped, a thin police officer got on it. He had horseshoe moustache style. With a smirk on his face, he pumped his chest and walked with assurance towards the passengers and barked emphatically, "Dear friends! Show me your identity cards." His sardonic smile and pronunciation of "dear friends" sounded as if to say, "I am calling you dear friends, but you must know that I am not your friend. You better not take it literally!"

While some passengers started to hand him their identity cards, a man of about forty years was sleeping and snoring loudly. The police officer roared, "My dear friend thinks he is in his bed!" He then gave the man a hard kick on the shin. The man jumped up and screamed out in pain. Confused, he wasn't aware of the police officer's presence. So, he grabbed his shin and was trying to figure out what happened. By the time he realized, a bony fist landed on his face, followed by a loud insult: "SAVAGE! You think you are in your house? Give me your id card RIGHT NOW or I'll kick YOUR ASS!" The man was bleeding and quivering out of fear and anger and handed his identity card to the police officer. He snatched it and insulted the man once again, "son of a bitch!" The rest of the passengers were shaking as they were getting their papers ready to hand them over to him as he approached them. They were all panicked. Nobody dared to say a word. An appalling silence invaded the bus. At the door, the apprentice was standing and addressed the police officer as "Boss! Can I help you?" "Boss" replied with attitude and in a contemptuous voice, "I AM DONE! Jerk!"

"Boss" was well-known at the border for his aggressive and unorthodox behavior towards passengers. He had no respect for elders or women. He was particularly hostile to young people. He rarely smiled. He always had a squeezed face like someone who just took some bitter pills. People used to say that he was embittered because his wife left him. He would beat her each time that he came back from work. He was known as a boozer and a terrible smoker. His nickname was also "the border chimney." He was pouring his bitterness on travelers.

So, as "Boss" was waddling towards the apprentice, he was also accompanied by a heavy smoke. Some passengers were coughing due to the smoke. His favorite cigarette was "Marlboro." It was said that "Boss" would sometimes stick his burning cigarette on the cheek of sleeping passengers to wake them up or kick them hard with his boots and then burst out in heavy laughter: "HA! HA! HA! HA!" "Boss" left the bus and made a peremptory gesture to the apprentice to follow him to his office. The apprentice acquiesced while running towards him. "Boss" did not like repeating himself. After all, he was the "Boss"! As the apprentice knew the expectation of "Boss," he followed him to the office and gave him some money to get back the passenger's identity cards. Ten minutes later, he came out with a broad smile. The first ordeal of the border was over. But, he did not return the passengers' identity cards, as he knew that the next ordeal was to pay off the custom officers. He wanted to use that strategy to press passengers to give more money to corrupt the custom officers. They also had to get their share of the cake, otherwise, they would require all the passengers' luggage be put down and opened for a so-called routine check. Failing to pay the minimum amount demanded, which was twenty-five thousand CFA francs, they would take all their time before coming to check the luggage and find the slightest pretext to block passengers at the border until they pay. So, the apprentice requested one thousand CFA francs from each passenger. This request was followed by a chorus of grumbles expressing disgust and protest, but it did not get any further. They gave out the amount requested. The apprentice then went back to the customs officer and handed over the money.

Meanwhile, the driver was snoring loudly under a tree on a bench. Apprentice went to wake him up. As the driver got up, he asked for some water to wash up his face. He then pulled out of his front pocket a package of cigarettes, took out one and lighted it and then mumbled something to the apprentice. Both went to the bus and a young customs officer on probation came and opened the barrier for them. They drove away. Other challenges were still ahead in Felikro.

Police and customs barriers and multiple checkpoints became part of the daily rituals that passengers had to go through before reaching their final destination.

Unsatisfied by their illicit gains, Felikro custom officers complained about their miserable salaries and decided to meet the President to negotiate for the improvement of their living conditions. Unfortunately, all their representatives who went to meet the President were all driving state-of-the art Mercedes. So, the President told them that any person living under miserable conditions could not drive such luxurious vehicles. They returned to their respective posts unsatisfied and continued to suck passengers' blood.

The social malaise and plague became regional and grew out of proportion. Material and moral decay were no longer a major concern for the people. The people had had enough of this nightmarish situation and were just trying to survive independence under the reign of their own sons and daughters who were often called the new gods of independence.

Gontan was sitting and observing all these hassles on the road. He had to obey just like the rest of the passengers. Salif was sitting by his side busy munching his cola-nut while acting as if he weren't aware of anything around him. He was apparently indifferent to the police and customs officers' misbehaviors. When Gontan finally told him that he couldn't believe that the police officers were absolutely corrupt and depraved, he replied that Gontan had not seen anything yet. That was just the tip of the iceberg, he added, before falling back asleep. Salif had become immune to all these misbehaviors. Apparently, he wasn't bothered at all or didn't want to express any sign of disappointment. His pride and sense of integrity seemed to have vanished in the midst of this depraved and decayed world.

All along his long journey to Felikro, Gontan experienced the same scenarios: constant requests for extra money to corrupt the police and custom officers, endless checkpoints, verbal and physical attacks on travelers. In short, no justice! He was speechless and was praying hard to reach his destination safely. As he was deeply involved in this reflection, he was trying to picture life in Morikro in his mind. He dared not ask Salif because he didn't want to be disappointed by what he might say about lifestyle in Morikro. He tried to drown these dark thoughts by painting a much beautiful picture of Morikro in his mind. He consoled himself by thinking that if other people were able to bear life and make it through, he could also make it. So, there was no need for too much concern.

After a five-hour drive, the apprentice shouted out "Morikro! Morikro in about fifteen minutes! Get ready Morikro! Morikro!" Gontan's heart started pounding at high speed. A little later, the bus stopped. Salif, Gontan and other passengers took their luggage and got off. Salif told Gontan that they just had to cross the road to get to his house, which was two blocks away.

As they were walking they saw a group of young people in a café. Sibiri recognized Salif and ran towards him. "Welcome! Welcome!" he said. When he got nearer, he recognized Gontan too. He shouted, "Oh! Man! Is this Gontan?" He then gave him a big hug. Both were really happy to meet after such a long time of separation.

Sibiri took Salif's bag and started bombarding Gontan with questions about Tiala, his family members, friends and old acquaintances. Gontan replied that they were all doing great when he left them.

When they got home, Salif's junior wife Alima offered them some water to drink. They rested a while, and then they took a bath. A little later, they were served with pounded cassava and plantain accompanied by spiced palm-nut soup with fish. Gontan enjoyed the food, as it was not really a common dish in his village.

"Where is Lamouni," Gontan asked?

"He is on the *togoda*," Sibiri replied. But Gontan didn't understand what he meant by *togoda*. His facial expressions clearly indicated that he was lost. Sibiri quickly explained that *togoda* meant "farmstead." He then added that Lamouni was doing pretty fine and that he should be coming in the evening for the weekend break.

Then Gontan asked with surprise, "Oh! So, you rest on the weekend?"

"Yes, every Sunday we take a rest and go shopping for the following week." Sibiri answered. Then, he added, "Life on the farm is really exciting, especially when you are accustomed to it. But, the first two weeks might be a little difficult for a newcomer as you are cut off from the village, and only surrounded by thick forest and you hear birdsongs and the cries of wild animals all the time. This can be really disturbing, especially for someone coming from the savannah. But you'll quickly adapt to the rhythm and even find life in the village a little boring sometimes."

Curious, Gontan asked, "So, you live in the forest? Do you sometimes see chimpanzees and lions?"

With a broad smile Sibiri replied, "Sometimes some chimps, but there are no lions in the forest. You mainly find lions in the savannah. Don't worry, we are here to guide and initiate you to the secret of the area. Tomorrow, Lamouni will take you around the village to show you a couple of places that you need to know. I'll go back to work and maybe if you want, you can join us on the farm. Salif was talking about hiring a temporary worker to weed his new coffee plantation. So, you really came in the nick of time."

As they were talking, Lamouni entered the yard with his bike. He had a lot of bananas tied to the carrier. He used to bring bananas to sell them on the market place and with the money earned; he would buy condiments and other stuffs for the week. Gontan and Sibiri went to help him untie his load and put it in the store, right at the entrance. Lamouni was smiling broadly as he saw Gontan. They hugged each other.

Lamouni rested a little bit and then went to take a warm bath. Lamouni used to be a shy person. He didn't like talking too much. However, lifestyle in Morikro changed him a lot. He became a little talkative. Further, he now spoke more Jula and some broken French. After his bath, he ate some fried rice and started a long conversation about lifestyle in Morikro in general and on the cocoa and coffee plantations in particular. As he was talking, Gontan was yawning. So, they cut it short and went to bed.

The following day, Sibiri went to the farm while Gontan and Lamouni made a quick tour of the local market to sell the banana that he brought home the previous day. As they were standing and talking while waiting for potential clients, a fair complexioned man of about forty years came closer and interrupted them very rudely, "HEY YOU GUYS! WHERE DID YOU GET THESE BANANAS?" Gontan was puzzled by the behavior and frowned at the man. But Lamouni stayed cool, as he knew the guy very well. His name was Marcel, a local youth leader, very famous in the village for his aggressive and xenophobic attitude

171

towards immigrants from the North. Lamouni just replied that he worked for Salif and that the bananas were from his plantation. Marcel didn't say anything else but just made a violent gesture full of disgust and hatred. Then, he left.

So, Lamouni briefed Gontan about such common verbal attacks on immigrants these days. He added that Marcel used to work in the marine as a cook. But given his discourtesy towards his foreign colleagues, he was kicked out. He owned a big and nice villa in the village, which he built when he was still on duty. Young people used to meet there, drink tea, smoke weed and party all day long.

Marcel would preach his principles of xenophobia to those jobless and lazy youth. He used to say that their fatherland was alienated by foreigners who took total control of the most fertile parts to the detriment of the natives. And yet, he was said to have inherited vast fertile lands from his father who was a Second World War Veteran. But he never exploited nor allowed any foreigner to farm it. Marcel used to say that one day his people would kick out all those foreigners by using all means at their disposal, including killing them.

Marcel's behavior added more to Gontan's shock. As they finally sold the bananas, they made a tour of the village and visited the main shops and video projection rooms. On weekends, Indian and Western movies were screened at fifty CFA francs per customer. Young people used to go there to while away the time as there was no movie theater in the neighborhood. After a long tour of the village, Gontan and Lamouni went back home where they met Salif, their boss.

The day was really short and it was already getting dark. So, Salif instructed Lamouni to take Gontan the next day to the plantation and to show him the plot that he would be weeding.

After eating dinner, Gontan and Lamouni decided to go to bed early to rest before the trip to the farm.

News from Felikro

The day that Gontan reached the farm was totally a day of real trial for him. He did not know how to handle the machete to weed properly. He didn't know how to distinguish some of the young plants from actual weeds. It was very tough for him. But Lamouni and Sibiri were there to encourage him and initiate him to weeding techniques. The following week, he took control of everything and was finally able to work without any guidance. Three weeks later, he decided to send a letter to his family back home as promised. His mother, his wife and his brother Pèret were all worried and did not know how to get in touch with him.

As usual on Sunday, Gontan, Lamouni and Sibiri returned to the village. Gontan didn't know how to read nor write, he therefore requested the services of Sibiri to write his first letter from abroad.

Dear Mom, brother and dear love,

I am writing this letter to inform you that I reached my final destination in good health. Thanks God, everything went on well. The road was very long and tough, but our ancestors and your blessing helped me get through. Don't worry! Nothing bad happened to me. I was even among the luckiest people on earth as I got a job on the bus, before leaving Tiala. Yes, I got a job! Can you imagine this? I sat near the very man who was the boss of my friends Lamouni and Sibiri. He gave me a job right away. So, I started working on his plantation for about three weeks now. Nothing special here, except that I live on the togoda, that is, the farm, in a thick forest. Yes! A thick forest! In the night, we are served with birdsongs as a lullaby and wild animal cries. I was a little scared at the beginning, but all that became a habit now.

My boss is a very kind person and he really cares about us. So far, we have been treated with respect. As I started working for about three weeks, I cannot send you money for the time being. But trust me! If things go as planned, I'll be sending you money.

Pèret, this is for you! I would like you to keep on working hard in order to promote our small business. I'll also be sending you money when I get paid. Take good care of your girlfriend. When the wedding approaches, let me know. It's true that I wanted to be there for the celebration, but things did not happen as we all wished. Distance cannot break our relationship as brothers and also as good friends. You know very well that you are my best friend. If you have any problem, please send me a message under the cover of Salif. He'll give it to me. Keep me posted about everything going on in the family. By the way, remember that I have some credits amounting to fifteen thousand CFAF with Gontoro, and I did not collect it. So, please talk to him and request the money. You can even use that money for the time being to enhance your business and also to cope with any emergency situation. So, for the time being, I don't have anything special to tell you. But I would be very pleased to hear from you so soon.

Now to Mom! Mom, as you know very well, I didn't forget your advice and support in the entire process of decision-making in order to come here at Morikro. You have been so supportive and understanding during the whole process. Mom, thank you very much. I just wanted you to know that I am doing very fine and that I miss you a lot. If you have any problem, please just write me a letter and I'll respond as quickly as possible. Keep on praying hard for me and for all of us. I love you Mom. Greet Papa Djibo and do convey to him my best regards.

To you my darling! I want you to know once more that I love you and that time and distance cannot and will not separate us. How is my little Tchiri doing? I know he is growing fast. How is he doing now? Tell him that I love him too.

Keep up the faith. And if you have any problem please write me a message now that you have my address. My first days in Morikro seem to give me more hope for the future. My trip was long, but I reached my final destination in good shape. My love, keep on praying for our reunion. I will work and pray hard to make it happen.

Dear Mom, brother and love, I know you would like to see my picture. Here is one that I took two days ago with Lamouni and Sibiri. It's a black and white photo, I hope you'll like it. Next time, I will go to the big city to take color pictures for you.

Once again, I love you all. To make a long story short, and to avoid giving more pain to Sibiri who offered to write this letter, I will leave it here hoping to hear from you very soon.

Love and divine blessing!

Gontan

* * *
*

The day Pèret received the mail was a great day of joy in the family. Everybody was very happy. Pèret decided to buy a rooster and a guinea fowl to celebrate the good news. He invited a couple of friends to share the meal and requested more blessings and prayers for his brother in this remote land. His business was thriving and life was much easier for the family.

Years passed. Gontan was still living in Morikro working on the coffee and cocoa plantations. He made enough money and planned to try his hand at trading as he used to do back in Tiala. Since he didn't know how to read and write, he decided to enroll in adult evening classes. He became the laughing stocks of some friends and workmates. They couldn't understand why he wanted to attend school at his age, just to read and write in French. Sibiri offered to help him in the process. From time to time, they spent nights together, with Sibiri helping him to read the alphabets and how to combine them. Gontan was really determined and in just a week, he was able to read his name, and a couple of words. His schoolteacher, Mr. Traoré offered to give him extra tutoring. The learning process was very intense and Gontan was persistent despite his heavy farm works. After five months of schooling, Gontan was able to write his own letters in somewhat intermediate French, and didn't need any specific assistance in communicating his feelings and thoughts in writing. He used to say to Sibiri and Lamouni that he wanted to take the primary school certificate exam as an independent candidate.

Sibiri would encourage him, but Lamouni used to laugh at him by saying, "Well, knowing how to read and write your name has nothing to do with writing an exam, especially the primary school certificate exam." But Gontan would just reply, "Where there is a will there is a way." Lamouni's bitterness was due to the fact that he dropped out of school much earlier for his poor performance. So, he couldn't understand why a grown-up like Gontan was determined to go to school and even dared to take the primary school certificate exam! Lamouni didn't like conversing in French because of this past poor school performance that apparently prohibited him from even trying to speak. He had a hang-up about his own failure.

As planned, after two years of intensive training, Gontan communicated in French and interacted with primary school students and civil servants in the village. He made good friends, notably Kwaku. Kwaku helped him a lot in his math exercises. Together, they talked in French, and reviewed their history, geography, biology and French lessons.

Gontan enrolled for the primary school certificate exam as envisioned. The day of the exam, it rained very heavily and all night long. Gontan woke up early in the morning, took a quick bath, had his breakfast and got ready to go to the examination center. He thought it was earlier, but when he got there, he found a lot of students with their parents. He also found other adults who came to take the exam. So, after all, he wasn't alone, he said to himself. He was a little worried as he didn't want to fail. Failure would be a bad sign and would be used against him as mockery, especially by his co-worker Lamouni.

An hour later, the examiners came around, and started reading out names to identify candidates. Once this routine was over, candidates went to their respective classrooms and took the seat bearing their registration numbers. A little later, the inspector came in with a sealed envelope, presented it to students and then opened it.

The first exam was a spelling test, accompanied with comprehension and grammar questions. Gontan was smiling broadly as he already knew the excerpt from a novel that was chosen for the test. He was especially concerned with the spelling test because his French wasn't that great, especially his French grammar. However, he managed to pull through. After that phase, the rest of the exam tests were much easier for him as he loved history, geography, biology and calculus. He was pretty sure he had done very well in the exam, but whenever asked about the results, he would just answer modestly, "Let's pray God and wait."

After the exam, Gontan returned to the farmstead to work. Lamouni kept on pestering him about the exam results but Gontan would just reply as usual, "Let's pray God. Everything is in the hands of God now." Yet in a very provocative way, Lamouni would add, "Well, you know, do not involve God in this exam thing! This is about your performance. So, if you did well, you should know it." Despite all of these provocative statements, Gontan managed to keep his cool. A month later, the school director summoned him to his office to inform him about his success and congratulated him for his great performance.

That year, the school presented ten independent candidates and six of them passed their exams with distinction. Gontan was one of them. So, the school director congratulated him and even offered to help him should he need any further assistance in his future learning plans. Gontan was overwhelmed with joy. Now that he passed his exam, he didn't know what to do next. When he informed his workmates, notably Sibiri and Lamouni, they smiled and shrugged. Sibiri congratulated him and even suggested that they organize a small party to celebrate the event. But Gontan preferred to be discreet, as he knew that very few people supported him in his adventure. Salif, his boss, also congratulated him and added: "I guess you are not going to leave us?" Gontan just replied smiling: "I don't think so. I feel very welcomed here and I consider this place my home."

A week later, Gontan sent a letter to his family back home, in Tiala to inform them about his success and future plans.

Dear brother,

I am writing this letter to inform you that I am doing very well here. My friends and workmates are doing pretty fine too. I hope you are also doing very well.

Guess what? I am personally writing you this letter because there is one thing I decided not to tell you until I made it. Yes, now I am through. I enrolled in evening classes and guess what? I took part in the primary school exam and I passed! Wow, I am very proud now and I intend to continue learning to improve my knowledge and understanding of the world. You know, we didn't get the chance to go to school because of what we all know. But thanks God, I decided to go to school to learn how to read and write in French. Everything went well. You may find this crazy, but I have always secretly aspired to be able to read one day. Now, that dream is achieved. Not only can I read, but I also passed my primary school certificate. I am pleasantly surprised by the way things went for me. I am really happy to share with you this specific moment of joy.

My future plans include buying my own land and owning a plantation. Yes, I want to have my own coffee and cocoa plantations. I know it's possible because I have been talking with some people around in the village and they told me that down in the south, there are very fertile lands for sale. I also wanted to start a small business, a small shop. But I don't want to hasten things. So, just pray God for me. Now that I know how to read and write, you will hear from me on a regular basis. I don't have to beg people any more in order to write letters for me. You know that when you don't know how to read and write you have to tell everything, even your personal secrets, to other people. Sometimes, they will propagate your personal affairs in bars and the next thing you know, the entire village is aware of your private life. Pèret, I also encourage you to read and write so that we can communicate easily.

Please, send my regards to Papa Djibo, and all our acquaintances. I am doing very fine as I said. I will send you

185

CFAF 100,000 in a couple of weeks to enhance your business and help my wife and son come over here. I want them to join me so that I can start my business. Alone, it's really very difficult. So, split the money and give CFAF 50,000 to my wife for her transportation. She and my son should come over here. You may give 10,000 to Mom and 10,000 to Djibo. You may keep the rest for yourself. I hope this will help enhance your business a little bit. Should you have any request, just send me a letter, and I will get back to you as soon as possible. Since I don't have a lot to say for today, I will stop here hoping to hear from you. I wish you all the best. Send my regards to all my friends, nephews and cousins.

Love and blessings,

Gontan

*

* * *

* * *
*

Three weeks later, Pèret received the letter from the local post office. He was totally surprised when he discovered that Gontan enrolled in school as an independent candidate and even passed his exam. "That was wonderful," he said. He quickly informed Gontan's wife, Djibo and their mother about Gontan's spectacular success. Pèret was not prepared to undertake such an adventure. He loved his little business the way it ran and believed his current knowledge of the market and the local communities were key factors in promoting his business. Now, he was wondering what would be the next surprise from his brother. He knew Gontan had always been very interested in political issues, but he was wondering whether he would want to play politics as people tended to see politicians as corrupt and dishonest. He loved to see his brother succeed but he didn't want him to be involved in local nor national politics. The villagers always perceived politics as a dishonest and dirty game.

Pèret recalled that, two years ago, the legislative elections held in the village turned into a total nightmare. Families were split up because of the fight over the money that politicians gave them to corrupt electors and buy their votes. Or perhaps, Gontan will just keep on with his trade and continue farming. After all, that's what he loved to do. He will leave politics to others. He smiled as his mind kept wondering about the future, his future, the future of his brother, the future of the entire family, the extended family.

The Man Who Called Himself 'Philosopher'

One day, Gontan decided to take a trip to the big city, the capital of Felikro. He wanted to visit Yakro, the big city next to the sea where *Mommy Watta*, the mermaid or the sea-goddess lived. He had heard that *Mommy Watta* would often emerge from the sea and lure young men. Any person who came across her could be blessed, depending on her mood. She might give him fortune, a piece of gold or a diamond. Yet, other people said that *Mommy Watta* could lure a young man into the sea and kill him. Other stories held that *Mommy Watta* often capsized fishers' boat when they violated fishing customs and practices. Gontan was not interested in meeting the sea-goddess.

He just wanted to visit Yakro to buy clothes, shoes and a couple of books. He dressed up to the nines and waited for the bus to Yakro. He also wanted to gauge the city to see where he could get good merchandise to start up his small shop one day.

After waiting a little while, the bus to Yakro arrived. There were still several empty seats available. He stepped on the bus, scanned it to identify the best seat. He hesitated for a couple of seconds and then sat next to a young bearded man, wearing a *dashiki* suit, and holding a folded newspaper in his left hand. He greeted him in French. The young man replied and then automatically opened his newspaper, flipped through it and began to read it silently. All of a sudden, the young man's face squeezed and he croaked, "A military coup in **GANDA-GULO!**"

Gontan couldn't help but scream back as he was from Ganda-Gulo.

"What? Did you say **GANDA-GULO?**" Gontan asked with his eyes wide-open.

"Yes, you heard me well. **GANDA-GULO!** Are you surprised?" The young man asked him.

"Well, yeah, kind of...I mean..." Gontan replied with a little embarrassment.

"Well, you shouldn't be surprised if you followed the news recently. There were social upheavals across the nation's capital, Mogodougou. The President became a total despot. Cronyism took over. He only appointed people from his tribe and friends in key leadership positions. His ministers, chief executive officers and directors were worshipped like gods. Officials who worked under their leadership were traumatized, but none of them dared say the truth." The young man added with disgust.

"Yeah, I'm from Ganda-Gulo, oh yeah, recent events showed that there was a real big turmoil. Yeah, despotism, that was the problem, I mean, that's the plague these days," Gontan said in an attempt to cover up the fact that he wasn't aware of the coup.

"Oh, by the way, I'm Samori. But you may call me the philosopher too." The young man introduced himself.

"Nice to meet you. I'm Gontan."

"Nice to meet you too." Samori replied while stroking his beard, and then returned to the military coup.

"It was the first time!" He said emphatically, "it was the first time that the people had had enough of their leader. They spent days in the streets demonstrating and asking him to step down. Independence became a nightmare for all of us. We fought for it and now our own brothers turned to looting our wealth. Instead of building our young nations, they were busy transferring funds to bank accounts in Switzerland. When the great famine hit Ganda-Gulo, President Mori, Ganda-Gulo's President himself came here to ask for support from his close friend, our President. It's really a pity that we cannot feed ourselves anymore. Even the most resourceful countries became champion beggars of international assistance. Greed! Not care for the people. Indeed, subsequent news revealed that instead, he took the money and celebrated his second wedding on a remote island while his people were perishing. Civil servants and trade unionists went on strike to denounce his misbehavior and oppressive laws. Through a decree, President Mori had drastically reduced their already meager salaries by twenty five percent. He had called the measure patriotism and those who opposed his decision were labelled as terrorists, traitors and scums plotting to undermine his own success as the Messiah. As part of his ploy, he also took a decree to change job specifications. Any job vacancy that required a Master's degree would be announced as requiring the O level while knowing that no high school students could perform such jobs. Since new graduates were desperate looking for jobs, they accepted the positions. Master's holders ended up earning wages initially meant for O level holders. When people complained about their wages, the Minister of Labor went on television and brandished the decree. He said emphatically "It is the law! Period! Take it or leave it!" That was the new way of accumulating and maximizing profit. Just like his peers, he saw himself as the sole and only enlightened leader to guide his people to the Promised Land. The Promised Land for him was of course, his accounts in Switzerland. When the people asked for the military to take power, he convened all the captains and generals and promoted them to higher ranks, distributed stars and transferred money into their bank accounts. Some of them kept silent and never said anything. But General Zana refused to tarnish his image and dignity. He responded to the people's call. We just have to hope that General Zana will be a better and visionary leader."

Gontan muttered, "It's really very sad that post-independence African leaders became the real enemies of their people. It's a calamity. In some countries, I heard that the leaders would line up their opponents and shoot them just like dogs. Others would even throw their enemies in the deep sea. How could you do that to your own people? How could a visionary leader do that? How could a caring leader do such things? I always wondered why."

"It's power, my brother. It is POWER and GREED. Remember, as the saying goes, "Absolute power corrupts absolutely." Africans need to unite; African youth need to wake up. But unfortunately, most promising African leaders, especially some young leaders, started to create associations to praise the corrupt leaders. They praise in their songs and speeches such corrupt leaders as the new Messiah, as monuments of African leadership. Some young African artists became modern day Griot. Not that I am against our noble griots. They are doing a great job. They are the guardians of our traditions and values. I am talking about those young artists who are only releasing albums singing and praising the chief executive officers, directors, ministers and our presidents and first-ladies. I am talking about those young artists who are releasing empty songs to praise the leaders for their poor vision and mediocrity. Associations or alliances of the friends of x, y or z have been popping up like wild and toxic fungi. Associations of young leaders with no vision or good policy! The only concerns of such associations are to earn easy money and instant gratification. Nothing else! So, the future is really bleak. It's the policy of divide and rule. When leaders realize that the youth are going to rebel against them, they always find a group of corrupt so-called 'intellectuals', myopic 'intellectuals' with no ethics and vision to divide the youth. Such young people who just completed their degrees in our universities are burning for the desire to make easy and quick money. They have become the new plague of our generations, the toxic and radioactive fungi. They are the ones that are going to jeopardize the future of Africa and the future of our fragile and young nations. Real evil comes from inside, not from outside. As the popular saying goes, "A house divided against itself cannot stand." We need real independence from the old and new generations of toxic and radioactive fungi, the ones that are poisoning our daily lives with toxic messages, toxic music, toxic songs, toxic associations, toxic ideas, and toxic discourses, all packaged like the real future of Africa. Trust me, there's no future in toxicity. To the best of my knowledge, poison is not food. Such young people and leaders have become radioactive and toxic. Very dangerous. Africa doesn't need such leadership. What we need is real conscious leaders, democratic leaders, leaders with vision and people-centered policies, leaders who care for real African independence, not leaders who transfer money to Swiss accounts while their people are starving. Our people need democracy, freedom, and of course independence from the current toxic and radioactive leaderships. We need now peaceful revolution, bloodless revolution like the one that just occurred in Ganda-Gulo. Getting rid of dictators who proclaimed themselves as founding fathers, the Messiah and only savior of the people; developing a really democratic constitution, that's what we need. Period.

Gontan was silent and was really impressed by Samori's vision of Africa. It was the first time for him to come across someone with such a vision of Africa. He even forgot that he was travelling and why he was travelling to the city. And then, he looked at Samori once again as if he really wanted to read his mind. Then, he asked: "What's the name of the newspaper you are reading?"

"It's *Africa's Tomorrow.*" Samori replied. "It's my favorite and only newspaper these days. I stopped reading all these toxic and radioactive newspapers. I stopped listening to all these toxic and radioactive media. *Africa's Tomorrow* is a newspaper with a vision. It interrogates African past, seeks to understand where we came from, what went wrong and how we can fix things. It proposes real solutions. *Africa's Tomorrow* doesn't sing and preach what the new leaders want to hear. It's a constructive newspaper. It explores Africa's past and rich history and teaches us what we can learn from that past, to transform the present and to better envision the future.

He then handed the newspaper to Gontan and told him to keep it.

Gonta sighed and said, "No matter how long the night, the sun will rise."

He thanked Samori for the gift. He opened the page where there was an article discussing the military coup in Ganda-Gulo and began to scan it.

Their bus was at the gate of the city of Yakro. They could read a welcome to Yakro sign: "Welcome to the city of marvels." As the bus drove by, Gontan saw people sitting by the roadside, selling items, conversing, carrying loads of fruit and bananas. He was shocked when he saw the piles of trash and muddy streets from his window. He saw people digging into the pile of trash, holding huge bags in their hands. As they were busy searching the rubbish piles, vultures were flying, jumping from place to place. The dogs were barking and pigs were oinking loudly at each other, apparently fighting over food. What shocked him was the young children in tattered clothes, digging energetically and pulling strange things from the garbage. He couldn't but wonder whether that spectacle was what the "city of marvels" was all about. Shocked and disgusted, he asked Samori, "What's that?"

Samori sighed, and answered while shrugging in disgust, "Well, that's Yama. It's the neighborhood of the poor, the disenfranchised, the marginalized, the people who were lured by the light and promise of the city. That's the tip of the iceberg. That's what our cities became. It is the city of the poor or ruralized cities. Then, the city of the rich, I mean the neighborhood occupied by the new leadership. Such neighborhoods were the residence of the colonial masters. The new elite live there now. They are busy building gated communities to keep their wealth and properties from the poor.

The new elite legislate and use the law to oppress the people. They destroy their young and fragile nations in the name of the law. They plunder institutional and state resources in the name of the law. The law has become the new God that kills innocent people. They traumatize and muzzle the people in the name of the law which has become synonym of injustice. The poor are left to fend for themselves, sometimes digging through rubbish and refuse to eat.

I apologize to even use the term "ruralized" because the kind of life that these people are living has nothing to do with life in rural areas. Life in rural areas is far much better than what you see here. Yeah, I should admit that our people left the rural areas because they couldn't sell the farm produce anymore at competitive prices. Our local markets have lately been invaded by imported goods. Worse, here in Felikro, we produce cocoa and coffee, but we do not even have a single factory to process and sell our own produce. That sums it all. A leadership with no vision!"

Gontan couldn't say anything else. He was so shocked by the news, and the sight that he was even hesitant to continue his exploration of Yakro. As the bus reached the station, he stepped out and walked towards the main market to meet Salif's brother, Moussa who was a trader in a different neighborhood called Pugon.

Pugon was a neighborhood where there were people from Ganda-Gulo, Sanandougou and Bamanandougou. It was a more diverse and better neighborhood than Yama. Gontan was warmly welcomed, served with fresh water and *fufu* or pounded yam accompanied with palm-nut soup and fish. He enjoyed it and then took a rest.

In the afternoon, Moussa took him around the main market where he bought shoes, clothes and a couple of goods for his future little shop. But he couldn't forget the image and spectacle he had encountered in Yama. Lifestyle in Pugon gave him more hope. He kept on meditating on the lengthy discourse by Samori, the young philosopher, and the contradiction of independent African states.

A flashback: He could still remember the echo of the philosopher's voice: toxic and radioactive leadership cannot save Africa. Yama cannot be the future of Africa nor will the toxic and radioactive leadership be the future of Africa.

Laws that cultivate, maintain and perpetuate injustice cannot be the future of Africa. Laws that deify leaders or encourage irresponsibility, the lack of accountability and transparency cannot be part of Africa's future.

Acknowledgements

Writing is a collective endeavor. I would like to take this opportunity to express my deepest gratitude to all the people who took their time to read the draft of this novel and provided comments and advice. My heartfelt thanks go to my wife Assetou Barry, Yacouba Tinguiri (cover drawing), Yaro Zakarya for their support and encouragement. Special thanks to Dr. Victor Doulou, Dieudonné Tamini, Dr. James Ngundi, Elizabeth Lang, Courtney Creek, Béatrice Goma, Bienvenu Akpakla, Lamoussa Gama, Johnny Sozi, Professor Christopher Wise, Professor Geoffrey Burkhart and Ms. Ana for your insightful comments and appreciation. As the African proverb goes, "I have no mouth to thank you." Thank you all for your caring support and guidance.

I would like to thank Createspace for creating this platform and for their guidance through their resources.

Glossary of Non-English Terms

Alamissa: Thursday

Allah Akbar: Arabic expression used to call for prayer. It means God is great.

Baaba yaa: The shout out for victory, especially when workers complete tilling an entire farm.

Dashiki suit: It is a colorful West African men's garment. The term means shirt in Yoruba.

Den-horon: A Mossi word for an honest and honorable person.

Djabi: Henna powder is used to dye hair, feet and hand palms. In West Africa, women use it to die their feet or the palm of their hands.

Djeliba: Djeli (griot or troubadour) and ba (big or great). The term means great griot.

Djirimbatiè: The place where a deceased person's body is placed. It is generally at the center of the common compound.

Djo-djiyan: Cooperative work on the in-law's farm. It is carried out as part of the bride price.

Fufu: Pounded yam

Fuuuuuuuu: Imitation of noise made by a falling object from the sky

Insha'Allah: Borrowed term from Arabic. It means if God pleases.

Joliba: Name of the river in the novel. It is made up of Joli which means blood and ba means great.

Kambô: Rhymed tilling technique accompanied by tom-tom beats and songs. Workers make successive noises with their hoes, which creates a harmonious rhythm.

Kana: It is a traditional hoe used to till a farm or garden.

Kari: Sunday

Kolo-mundo: Literally rolled up chicken. It is the chicken given to in-laws as part of the bride price.

Kudjèma: Collaborative or mutual farm work. It is done on a rotating basis. Members are often friends or relatives.

Laason: It is a ceremony carried out ten days after the funerals.

Labara-Nkondo: God on High or the Supreme being

Lansara: The white man

Mèwara: It literally means massaging the body. It is part of the formalities before any intimate relations between future couples to avoid any bad luck that could harm the woman's reproductive capacities.

Mommy Watta: The sea-goddess

Muntolo: Harvest feast. It is a ceremony organized at the end of harvests to thank the ancestors and the gods.

N'yé-Yiranè: It means tradition. It literally means born and found.

Néré: African locust bean tree

Simu: Generally millet flour mixed with water and honey or sugar. It is used as drink during ceremonies or sacrifices.

Taguma-paa: Bride price

Tiéla: The mediator. The tiéla is the workers' manager. Here the tiéla organizes and coordinates the collaborative farm work.

Tô: Millet, sorghum or corn paste. It is cooked and eaten with any kinds of sauce.

Togoda: Farmstead

Yii: Traditional beer made from sorghum

Yimbo: Child naming ceremony

Yuyu: Exclamation expressing joy. It is generally performed by women.

* 9 7 8 0 6 1 5 9 8 1 6 9 7 *